THE TASTE OF
CHINA

Frederic Lebain   Jean Paul Paireault

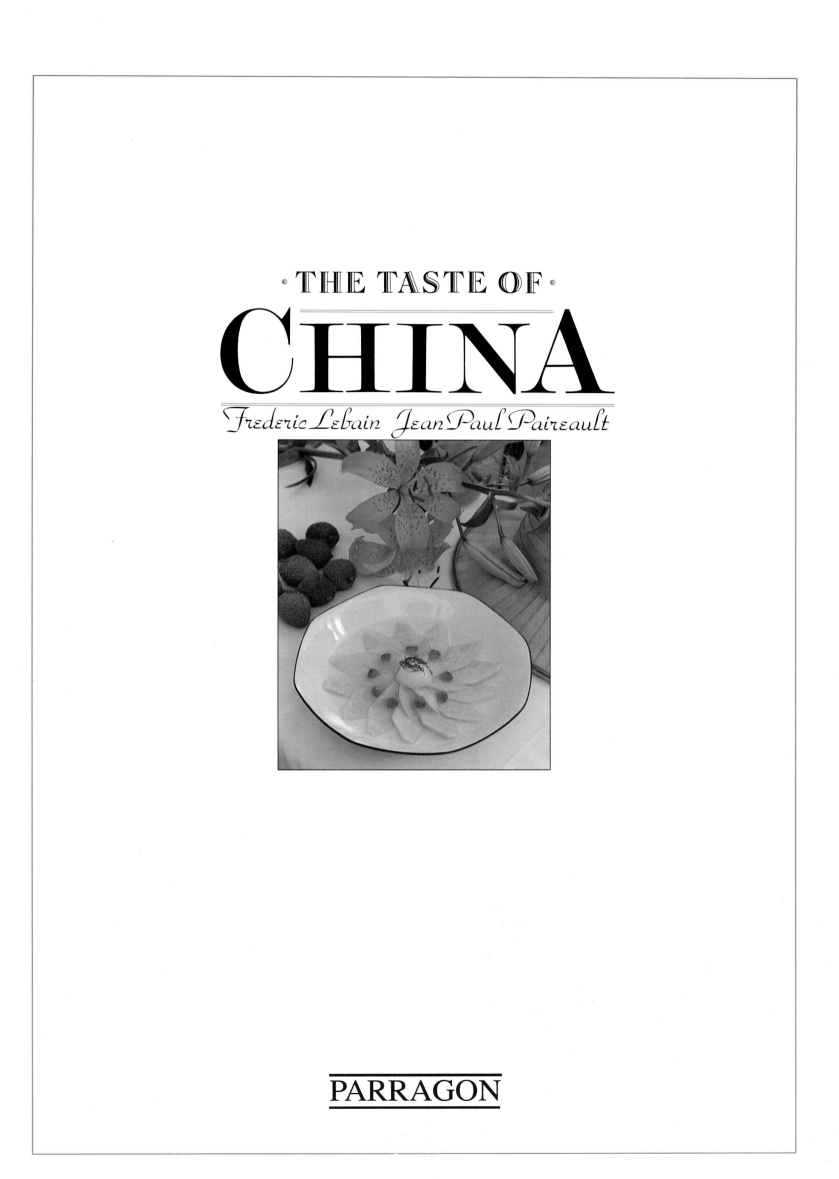

PARRAGON

Compiled by Frédéric Lebain and Jean-Paul Paireault
Photographed by Jean-Paul Paireault
Designed by Sally Strugnell and Alison Jewell
Adapted and Translated by Lynn Jennings-Collombet

Acknowledgements

The publishers would like to thank the following for their valuable assistance and cooperation in the production of this book:

Madame Bayle, at Mas Le Plan in Lourmarin, for facilities for location photography.
The shopkeepers of Lourmarin and Pertuis for their special efforts to obtain and provide a variety of fresh and attractive fish, meats and general provisions.
Morcrette, and Villeroy and Boch for the loan of glassware and plates.
Cine Photo Provence, in Aix-en-Provence for film processing.
Kettie Artigaud for her help with general styling and furnishing.
Kathleen Jennings for her patience and help throughout the adaptation and translation of this book.
Monsieur Remande, director of l'Ecole Supérieure de Cuisine in Paris.
Chef Xavier Vallero and Chef Eric Trochon for permission to use a selection of their recipes.
Also to Monsieur and Madame Lebain, Monsieur David and Madame Marie-Solange Bezaunt, Madame Chardot, and Monsieur Bernard Bouton of Sougé.

2196
© 1990 Coombe Books
This edition published in 1993 by Coombe Books
for Parragon Book Service Ltd.,
Unit 13-17, Avonbridge Trading Estate
Atlantic Road, Avonmouth, Bristol BS11 9QD
Printed in Spain
ISBN 1-85813-575-3

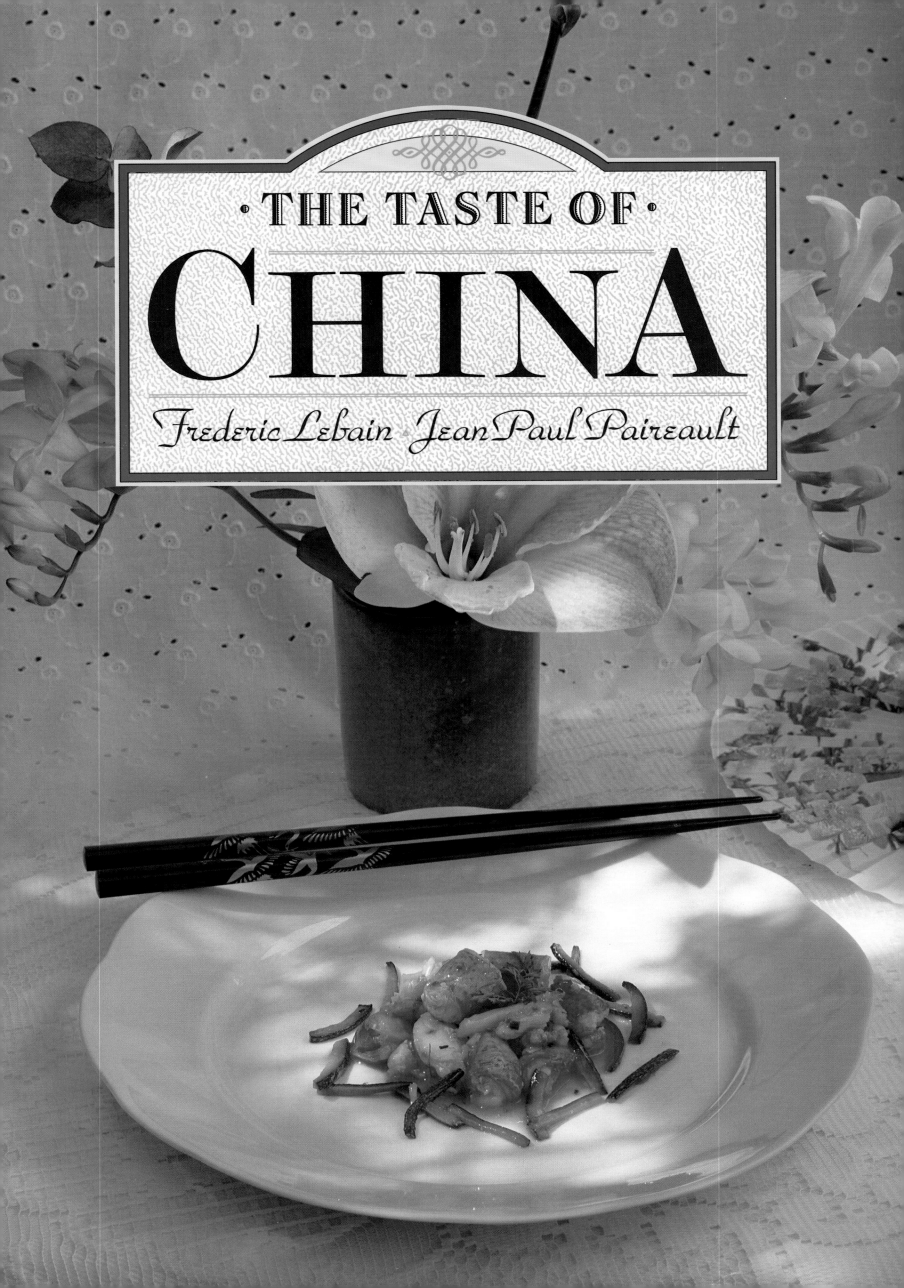

THE TASTE OF
CHINA

Frederic Lebain Jean-Paul Paireault

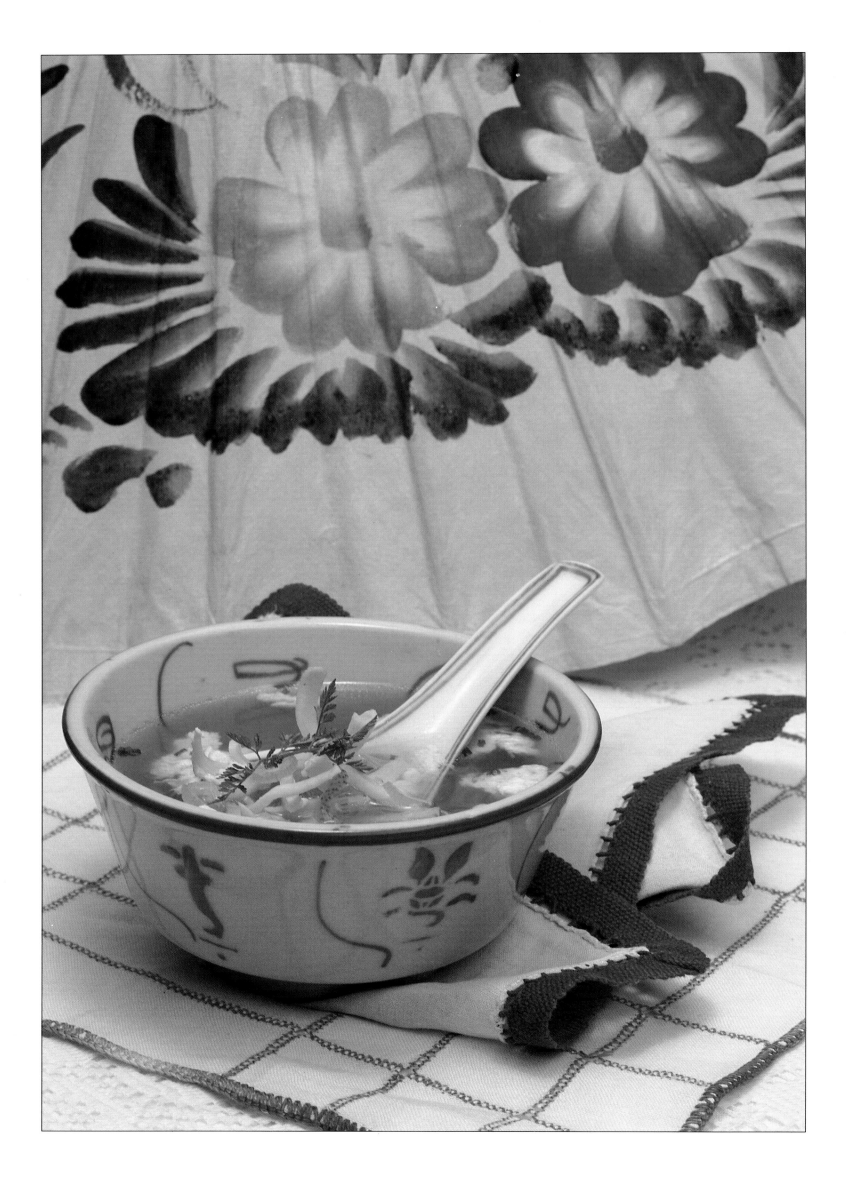

Introduction

In the West we talk blithely of 'Chinese cooking', as though such a vast country as China might possess one homogenous cuisine. In truth, extreme variations in climate and geography have provided such a wide variety of available ingredients, that many different regional cooking styles have developed. Nevertheless they have three distinct features in common, and these could be said to characterise a uniform style of Chinese cooking.

The first of the common features is the use of the technique of stir-frying, in which the ingredients are cooked quickly in a small amount of oil at high temperatures. The secret of good stir-frying is preparing all the ingredients carefully beforehand and then cooking them in a particular order, so that in the finished dish each ingredient is cooked and yet retains all its taste, goodness and texture.

The importance of texture in Chinese cooking is the second of its common features. After cooking, vegetables should retain all their crispness and rice and noodles should still have 'bite'. The Chinese also use some ingredients which have very little taste in themselves specifically to add different textures to dishes. These include ingredients which are familiar and easily available to Westerners, such as bamboo shoots, water chestnuts and cellophane noodles, and others which are both less readily available and perhaps less immediately appealing to Western palates, such as shark's fin, bird's nest and hair seaweed.

The third common feature is the use of dried foodstuffs. Dried mushrooms, seafood, bean curd, noodles of many varieties, tangerine peel, dates, sausages and, of course, spices are all extremely important in Chinese cooking. Originally developed to preserve foods for out-of-season use, dried products are now used throughout the year in Chinese cooking because they add a fuller flavour to the dish, than the equivalent fresh product.

Beyond these common features, Chinese cooking can be divided into four main styles. Southern or Cantonese cooking, which is perhaps the best known in the West, is characterised by subtle flavours and clear sauces, with rice as the staple accompaniment. Eastern or Shanghai cooking is also lightly seasoned but is much richer, because the meat is marinated beforehand and strongly flavoured stocks are used. Western or Szechuan cooking is very highly seasoned and intensely flavoured, the area being famous for its peppercorns and chillies. Finally, Northern or Peking cooking uses minimal seasonings, shows Mongolian influences in the popularity of lamb dishes and favours steamed or roasted breads or noodles as an accompaniment.

Western interest in Chinese cooking is relatively recent and has come about largely through the restaurants initially established by immigrants to service their own communities. Increased travel by Westerners to the East and a growing realisation amongst the health conscious of the benefits of the Chinese style of cooking have increased its popularity. The initial interest has now been followed by a demand from cooks for the means to experiment at home and authentic Chinese ingredients are becoming more readily available not just in specialist shops but even in supermarkets.

The Taste of China takes all the characteristics of Chinese cooking, both national and regional, and turns them into dishes which are sometimes classic and sometimes inventive interpretations of the classics, inventiveness and individuality being truly representative of the nature of Chinese cooking. The result is a mouthwatering collection of recipes, each presented in an easy-to-follow step-by-step format and accompanied by a colour photograph of the finished dish. By not confining itself to one particular style or technique, the broad scope of this book provides the cook with a true taste of China.

—————— SERVES 4 ——————

CRAB SOUP WITH GINGER

*This delicately flavoured soup, with fresh crab and a hint of ginger,
is perfect for serving at a special dinner.*

Step 2

Step 2

Step 2

☐ 1 carrot, chopped   ☐ 1 onion, chopped   ☐ ½ leek, chopped
☐ 1 bay leaf   ☐ 2 medium-sized crabs   ☐ 700ml/1¼ pints fish stock
☐ 1-inch piece of fresh ginger root, chopped
☐ 1 tsp sake   ☐ Salt and pepper

1. Make a vegetable stock by putting the carrot, onion, leek and bay leaf into a saucepan with a large quantity of water. Bring to the boil and add the crabs. Allow to boil briskly for 20 minutes or until cooked.

2. Remove the crabs when cooked and allow to cool. Once cooled, break off the pincers and break the joints, cut open the back and open the claws. Carefully remove all the crab meat.

3. Bring the fish stock to the boil and add the ginger, sake and the crab meat. Boil for 15 minutes.

4. Check the seasoning, adding salt and pepper as necessary. Serve very hot.

☐ TIME   Preparation takes about 40 minutes and cooking takes approximately 35 minutes. It takes about 30 minutes for the crab to cool, before you can comfortably remove the meat with your fingers.

☐ CHECKPOINT   Allow plenty of time for opening the crab and removing all the meat. If time does not permit preparing fresh crab, use canned crab meat.

☐ COOK'S TIP   Prepare the soup the day before serving. If allowed to rest overnight, the flavours of the soup develop deliciously. Reheat gently just before serving.

☐

OPPOSITE

CRAB SOUP
WITH GINGER

───── SERVES 4 ─────

CHINESE RAVIOLI

Steamed Chinese ravioli with a stuffing of pork and Chinese leaves.

Step 2

Step 3

Step 4

□ 450g/1lb pork, finely diced   □ 225g/8oz Chinese leaves, finely sliced   □ 1 spring onion, chopped   □ 1 tbsp soy sauce   □ Salt and pepper   □ 16 wonton wrappers (Chinese ravioli)   □ 1 egg, beaten   □ 1 tsp sesame oil

1. In a bowl, mix together the pork, Chinese leaves, spring onion and soy sauce. Season with salt and pepper. Leave to marinate for 30 minutes, stirring occasionally.

2. Peel off the wonton wrappers one by one and place a little of the drained stuffing on each. Try not to get any stuffing on the edges of the wrappers.

3. Brush the edges of the wrappers with the beaten egg.

4. Fold them in half, pushing the stuffing into the centre and pushing out any trapped air. Seal the edges well with your fingers and then cut off any excess dough with a knife or a pastry cutter.

5. Cook the ravioli on a damp tea towel in a Chinese steamer for approximately 15 minutes. Turn over once during cooking and brush with the sesame oil.

6. If you have any stuffing left over, stir-fry it quickly in a little hot oil and serve with the ravioli.

□ TIME   Preparation takes about 20 minutes and cooking takes approximately 25 minutes.

□ CHECKPOINT   It is very important to seal the edges of the ravioli firmly before steaming, otherwise the stuffing will leak out.

□ COOK'S TIP   Any excess dough trimmed off in Step 4, can be cut into small pieces and added to a soup.

□

OPPOSITE

CHINESE
RAVIOLI

—— SERVES 4 ——

ABALONE SOUP

*Canned abalone cooked in fish stock and flavoured with
oyster and soy sauces – absolutely delicious.*

Step 2

Step 2

□ 700ml/1¼ pints fish stock   □ 6 canned abalone + 2 tbsps
reserved juice   □ ½ spring onion, chopped   □ 1 tbsp soy sauce
□ ½ tbsp oyster sauce   □ 1 egg white   □ Salt and pepper

1. Heat together the fish stock, the reserved abalone juice, spring onion, soy sauce and the oyster sauce.

2. Cut the canned abalone first into thin slices and then into matchsticks. Add to the stock and simmer gently for 15 minutes.

3. Beat the egg white lightly and then stir it gradually into the boiling soup.

4. Season with salt and pepper to taste and serve.

□ TIME   Preparation takes about 5 minutes and cooking time is approximately 15 minutes.

□ VARIATION   The fish stock can be replaced by chicken stock.

□ WATCHPOINT   The egg white should be lightly beaten and added to the boiling soup slowly, so that it thickens immediately.

OPPOSITE

ABALONE SOUP

SPRING ROLLS

*Stuffed spring rolls, served slightly chilled make
a wonderful pre-dinner appetizer.*

Step 7

Step 7

Step 7

☐ 1 large pork chop, cooked   ☐ 100g/4oz chicken meat, cooked
☐ 1 tsp soy sauce   ☐ 1 tsp sugar   ☐ 2 tbsps sesame oil
☐ 50g/2oz bamboo shoots, blanched   ☐ 225g/8oz bean sprouts
☐ 1 Chinese mushroom, soaked for 15 minutes in warm water and
sliced thinly   ☐ 1 tsp cornflour, combined with a little water
☐ 18 square sheets rice paper, soaked in water

FOR THE SAUCE

☐ 2 tbsps water   ☐ Juice of ½ lemon   ☐ 1 tsp sugar   ☐ 1 clove
garlic, chopped   ☐ 2 tbsps each carrot and courgette, cut into
thin strips   ☐ 2 tbsps fish sauce

1. Remove the pork meat from the bone and cut into thin strips.

2. Cut the chicken meat into thin strips.

3. Mix the two meats together with the soy sauce, sugar and 1 tbsp of the sesame oil. Allow to marinate until required.

4. Heat the remaining sesame oil in a wok and stir-fry the bamboo shoots, bean sprouts and mushroom. Cook until tender.

5. Add the meat mixture and the marinade to the wok. Stir well and heat through.

6. Thicken the contents of the wok by stirring in the cornflour. Set the wok aside and allow the contents to cool completely.

7. Drain the rice paper sheets. Place a little stuffing on each of the sheets. Fold up the bottom half of each sheet, then fold over the side flaps. Finally, roll up each sheet, beginning at the bottom where the stuffing is visible, and seal the edges by brushing lightly with water. Allow the rolls to dry. Chill in the refrigerator.

8. Mix together the sauce ingredients and serve with the rolls.

☐ TIME   Preparation takes about 25 minutes and cooking takes approximately 15 minutes.

☐ COOK'S TIP   If time permits, it is better to stir-fry the bean sprouts, mushrooms and bamboo shoots separately and then mix them all together just before placing the stuffing on the rice paper.

☐ SERVING IDEA   Serve with shredded lettuce leaves.

☐

OPPOSITE

SPRING ROLLS

————— SERVES 4 —————

CHICKEN AND SWEETCORN SOUP

*This soup uses baby corn on the cob and chicken
and is flavoured with ginger and soy sauce.*

Step 2

Step 3

Step 4

□ 150g/6oz canned sweetcorn □ 700ml/1¼ pints chicken stock □ 2 chicken breasts, cooked □ 12 baby corn on the cob □ 1-inch piece of fresh ginger root, chopped □ 2 tbsps light soy sauce □ Pinch monosodium glutamate □ Few drops chilli sauce □ Salt and pepper

1. Place the canned sweetcorn in a food processor with 100ml/4 fl oz of the chicken stock. Process until smooth.

2. Strain the purée through a sieve, pushing it through with the help of a spoon.

3. Cut the chicken into thin slices and stir them into the remaining stock, in a saucepan.

4. Stir in the sweetcorn purée.

5. Add the baby corn and bring to the boil. Simmer for 15 minutes. Add the ginger, soy sauce, and monosodium glutamate. Continue cooking for another 10 minutes.

6. Add a few drops of chilli sauce. Check the seasoning, adding salt and pepper if necessary and serve.

□ TIME   Preparation takes about 5 minutes and cooking takes approximately 25 minutes.

□ COOK'S TIP   Prepare the soup the day before serving to give the flavours time to develop.

□ VARIATION   Creamed corn can be used instead of the processed corn.

□

<u>OPPOSITE</u>

CHICKEN AND
SWEETCORN
SOUP

—— SERVES 4 ——

RICE SOUP

*A tasty, economical soup which
uses leftover meat.*

Step 3

Step 4

▢ 4 dried Chinese mushrooms, soaked in warm water for 15 minutes ▢ 700ml/1¼ pints duck stock ▢ 1 spring onion, chopped ▢ 2 tbsps canned sweetcorn ▢ 100g/4oz leftover meat, chopped into small cubes ▢ Pinch ground ginger ▢ 1 tbsp sake ▢ 1 tbsp soy sauce ▢ Salt and pepper ▢ 100g/4oz cooked rice

---

1. Drain the mushrooms and slice thinly, discarding the stalks.

2. Place the mushrooms in a saucepan with the duck stock and the spring onion.

3. Add the sweetcorn, meat, ginger, sake, soy sauce, and salt and pepper to taste. Bring to the boil and simmer briskly for 10 minutes.

4. Stir in the rice and cook for 1 minute. Check the seasoning, adjusting as necessary, and serve.

▢ TIME   Preparation takes about 5 minutes and cooking takes approximately 12 minutes.

▢ VARIATION   You can use any sort of meat in this soup: beef, chicken, pork, etc.

▢ CHECKPOINT   If you do not like your rice too soft, add half-cooked rice, which will then finish cooking in the soup.

▢

OPPOSITE

RICE SOUP

SERVES 4

TURKEY SOUP WITH BLACK MUSHROOMS

*An unusual blend of flavours which makes a
tasty, warming soup.*

Step 1

Step 1

□ 150g/6oz turkey breast   □ 1 tbsp sesame oil   □ 50g/2oz dried
black Chinese mushrooms, soaked for 15 minutes in warm water
□ 700ml/1¼ pints chicken stock   □ 1 tbsp soy sauce   □ 1 slice
fresh root ginger   □ Salt and pepper

1. Cut the turkey meat into slices and then into small cubes.

2. Heat the sesame oil in a wok and stir-fry the meat until brown.
Remove from the pan and drain off all the excess oil.

3. Cook the mushrooms in boiling, salted water for 10 minutes. Rinse
and drain well.

4. Place the mushrooms in a saucepan with the stock. Stir in the meat,
soy sauce, ginger and salt and pepper to taste.

5. Bring to the boil and then simmer gently for 15 minutes.

6. Serve the soup piping hot.

□ TIME   Preparation takes about 8 minutes and cooking takes
approximately 35 minutes.

□ SERVING IDEA   Sprinkle the soup with 1 tbsp chopped fresh
chives before serving.

□ CHECKPOINT   Don't forget to remove the slice of ginger before
serving.

OPPOSITE

**TURKEY SOUP
WITH BLACK
MUSHROOMS**

───── SERVES 4 ─────

BEEF AND NOODLE SOUP

*Marinated beef is sliced and cooked in beef stock with noodles to
make a rich and extremely filling soup.*

Step 1

Step 1

□ 225g/8oz fillet of beef   □ ½ tsp chopped garlic   □ 1 spring
onion, chopped   □ 2 tbsps soy sauce   □ Salt and pepper
□ 225g/8oz fresh noodles   □ Few drops sesame oil
□ 700ml/1¼ pints beef stock   □ Few drops chilli sauce
□ 1 tbsp chopped chives

1. Cut the beef into thin slices. Sprinkle the chopped garlic and spring onion over the meat. Finally, sprinkle over the soy sauce and season with salt and pepper. Marinate the meat for 15 minutes.

2. Cook the noodles in boiling, salted water to which a few drops of sesame oil have been added. Rinse them in cold water and set aside to drain.

3. Bring the beef stock to the boil and add the beef and the marinade. Simmer gently for 10 minutes.

4. Stir in the noodles, season with a few drops of chilli sauce and simmer just long enough to heat the noodles through.

5. Serve with chives sprinkled over the top.

□ TIME   Preparation takes about 5 minutes, marinating time is 15 minutes and cooking takes approximately 12 minutes.

□ VARIATION   If you used a marrowbone to make the stock, add a little chopped beef marrow to the soup, just before serving.

□ WATCHPOINT   Do not overcook the noodles; they should still be quite firm at the end of Step 2.

□

OPPOSITE

BEEF AND
NOODLE SOUP

——— SERVES 4 ———

CHICKEN AND BEAN SPROUT SOUP

A quickly-prepared, aromatic soup with chicken and bean sprouts.

Step 2

Step 3

□ 225g/8oz cooked boneless chicken	□ 300g/12oz bean sprouts
□ 700ml/1¼ pints chicken stock	□ 1 tbsp white wine vinegar
□ 2 tsps sugar □ 2 tbsps soy sauce	□ 1 tbsp chopped onion
□ 2 shallots, chopped	□ Salt and pepper

1. Cut the chicken meat into small cubes.

2. Put the bean sprouts and the stock into a saucepan and bring to the boil.

3. Reduce the heat and add the meat, vinegar, sugar, soy sauce, onion, shallots and salt and pepper to taste.

4. Stir well and cook the soup for 15 minutes over a moderate heat. Serve hot.

□ TIME   Preparation takes about 4 minutes and cooking takes approximately 15 minutes.

□ VARIATION   The chopped onion could be replaced with spring onion.

□ CHECKPOINT   The bean sprouts should still be slightly crunchy when the soup is cooked.

□

OPPOSITE

CHICKEN AND
BEAN SPROUT
SOUP

--- SERVES 4 ---

FISH AND RICE SOUP

*This fish soup is delicately flavoured with ginger and contains
finely sliced fish and rice.*

Step 2

Step 2

☐ 700ml/1¼ pints fish stock   ☐ 1 tbsp soy sauce   ☐ 1 slice fresh
ginger root, chopped   ☐ 300g/12oz fresh cod or haddock fillet
☐ ½ tsp cornflour, combined with a little water
☐ 100g/4oz rice, part-cooked   ☐ Salt and pepper

1. Heat together the fish stock, soy sauce and ginger.

2. Cut the fish fillet first into very thin slices and then into strips.

3. Stir the cornflour into the stock and simmer gently for 10 minutes.

4. Stir in the drained, precooked rice and cook for 5 minutes.

5. Remove from the heat and add the fish.

6. Allow the fish to cook for several minutes in the hot soup. Check the
seasoning, adding salt and pepper as necessary and serve immediately.

☐ TIME   Preparation takes about 5 minutes and cooking takes
approximately 15 minutes.

☐ VARIATION   Any variety of fish could be used in this recipe, but
remember to slice it very thinly.

☐ COOK'S TIP   The rice should have been precooked in boiling,
lightly salted water for approximately 3 minutes, before being used in
this recipe.

☐

OPPOSITE

FISH AND RICE
SOUP

SERVES 4

CHINESE OMELETTE

A chicken, ham and prawn omelette,
flavoured with chopped chives.

Step 1

Step 2

□ 8 eggs, beaten   □ 2 slices ham, chopped   □ 150g/6oz cooked chicken meat   □ 8 cooked prawns, peeled and chopped   □ 1 tbsp chopped chives   □ ½ tbsp soy sauce   □ 2 tbsps oil   □ Salt and pepper

1. Mix together the eggs, ham, chicken and prawns.

2. Stir in the chives and soy sauce. Check the seasoning, adding salt and pepper to taste.

3. Heat the oil in a frying pan. Add the omlette mixture.

4. Gently stir the omelette with a fork as it is cooking.

5. Fold over first one side of the omelette and then the other, using the tines of the fork to shape it. Serve hot.

□ TIME   Preparation takes 8 minutes and cooking takes approximately 6-10 minutes.

□ VARIATION   This omelette can be made with a variety of herbs and cooked meats.

□

OPPOSITE

CHINESE
OMELETTE

FISH SOUP WITH SURPRISE WONTONS

*Chinese ravioli stuffed with prawns and cooked
in a fish-flavoured soup.*

Step 4

Step 4

Step 4 ∟

☐ 700ml/1¼ pints fish stock   ☐ 12 fresh prawns, peeled and heads removed, peelings and heads set aside   ☐ 1 tbsp oil   ☐ ½ tsp chopped parsley   ☐ Pinch chopped garlic   ☐ Salt and pepper   ☐ 12 wonton wrappers   ☐ 1 egg, beaten   ☐ 1 tbsp soy sauce

1. In a saucepan, bring the fish stock to the boil together with the reserved heads and peelings from the prawns. Boil gently for 15 minutes. Strain through a fine sieve, reserving only the stock.

2. Heat the oil in a wok and stir-fry four of the prawns, cut into small pieces, together with the parsley, garlic and salt and pepper to taste. Allow to cool.

3. Spread out the wonton wrappers and place a little of the above stuffing on each one.

4. Brush the beaten egg all around the edges of the dough. Fold one side over onto the other, cut the ravioli into the desired shape and seal well by pinching the edges together firmly. Set the ravioli aside to rest for 10 minutes.

5. Bring the stock back to the boil, then add the remaining prawns and the soy sauce. Pinch once more round the edges of the ravioli, then slip them into the stock. Season with salt and pepper and simmer briskly for 5 minutes.

6. Serve piping hot.

☐ TIME   Preparation takes about 20 minutes, resting time for the ravioli is 10 minutes and cooking takes approximately 20 minutes.

☐ VARIATION   You could replace the prawns in this recipe with any type of shellfish.

☐ WATCHPOINT   Pinch together the edges of the ravioli very firmly, so that none of the stuffing escapes during cooking. Do not, however, brush on too much egg, or the dough will soften.

☐

OPPOSITE

FISH SOUP WITH
SUPRISE
WONTONS

—— SERVES 4 ——

CLEAR CHICKEN SOUP
WITH EGG

*A tasty soup based on chicken stock with lots of flavour-enhancing
ingredients and served with a poached egg.*

Step 2

Step 3

Step 4

□ 4 dried Chinese mushrooms, soaked for 15 minutes in warm water
□ 1 tbsp coarse sea salt   □ 1 tbsp wine vinegar   □ 1 bay leaf
□ 4 eggs   □ 700ml/1¼ pints chicken stock   □ 1 onion, chopped
□ 10 chives   □ 1 tbsp soy sauce   □ Few drops chilli sauce
□ Salt and pepper

1. Cook the mushrooms in boiling, salted water for 15 minutes, rinse in fresh water and set aside to drain. Cut them into thin slices.

2. Set a large saucepan of water to boil, with the sea salt, vinegar and bay leaf.

3. When the water is boiling, reduce to a gentle simmer and carefully break in the eggs one at a time.

4. Poach the eggs for 1 minute and then remove them from the boiling water with a slotted spoon. Drain on a tea towel.

5. Heat the stock in a saucepan with the onion, bring to the boil and simmer for 10 minutes.

6. Strain the stock through a fine sieve, discarding the onion. Check the seasoning, adding salt and pepper as necessary.

7. Bring the stock back to the boil and add the mushrooms, chives, soy sauce and a few drops of chilli sauce. Cook for 10 minutes. One minute before serving add the eggs.

□ TIME   Preparation takes about 10 minutes, rehydrating the mushrooms 15 minutes and cooking takes approximately 10 minutes.

□ VARIATION   Replace the chicken eggs with quail eggs.

□ COOK'S TIP   The vinegar is not used in this recipe to add flavour, but to prevent the eggs turning brown.

□

OPPOSITE

**CLEAR CHICKEN
SOUP WITH EGG**

—— SERVES 4 ——

BAMBOO SHOOT SOUP

*A very decorative soup. Beaten egg sieved into
the hot soup gives a very special effect.*

Step 5

Step 5

Step 5

☐ 100g/4oz bamboo shoots, cut into thin matchsticks ☐ 4 dried
Chinese black mushrooms, soaked for 15 minutes in warm water
☐ 700ml/1¼ pints chicken stock ☐ 1 tbsp wine vinegar
☐ 2 tbsps light soy sauce ☐ Salt and pepper
☐ ½ tsp cornflour, combined with a little water
☐ 1 egg ☐ 10 chives

1. Blanch the bamboo shoots in boiling, salted water for 3 minutes.
Rinse and set aside to drain.

2. Cook the mushrooms in boiling, salted water for 10 minutes. Rinse
and set aside to drain.

3. Bring the stock to the boil and add the bamboo shoots, mushrooms,
vinegar and soy sauce and season with salt and pepper to taste. Cook
for 10 minutes.

4. Stir in the cornflour and bring the soup slowly back to the boil.

5. Reduce the heat. Beat the egg thoroughly. Place the beaten egg in a
sieve and add to the soup by shaking the sieve back and forth over the
hot soup.

6. Add the chives to the soup and serve piping hot.

☐ TIME   Preparation takes about 5 minutes and cooking takes
approximately 30 minutes.
☐ CHECKPOINT   Make sure the soup is boiling hot before adding
the beaten egg.
☐ COOK'S TIP   Try to buy fresh chives for this soup, as they have a
much better flavour than dried chives

☐

OPPOSITE

BAMBOO SHOOT
SOUP

LAMB AND NOODLE SOUP

*A hearty soup based on lamb stock with
mushrooms and lamb meat.*

Step 1

☐ 100g/4oz transparent noodles ☐ 6 dried Chinese mushrooms,
soaked for 15 minutes in warm water ☐ 700ml/1¼ pints lamb stock,
skimmed ☐ 150g/6oz lamb meat, sliced ☐ 1 tbsp soy sauce
☐ Few drops chilli sauce ☐ Salt and pepper

1. Break the transparent noodles into small pieces and cook them in
boiling, salted water for 20 seconds. Rinse them in fresh water and set
aside to drain.

2. Cook the mushrooms in boiling, lightly salted water for 15 minutes,
rinse them in fresh water and set aside to drain.

3. Cut the mushrooms into thin slices.

4. Heat the lamb stock in a saucepan and add the lamb, mushrooms,
soy sauce and a few drops of chilli sauce.

5. Season with salt and pepper and simmer gently for 15 minutes.

6. Stir in the drained noodles and simmer just long enough for the
noodles to heat through. Serve immediately.

☐ TIME   Preparation takes about 5 minutes, rehydrating the
mushrooms about 15 minutes and cooking takes approximately 30
minutes.

☐ VARIATION   Use fresh Chinese noodles instead of the transparent
noodles.

☐ COOK'S TIP   If the noodles are too hard to break with your
fingers, use a serrated knife to cut them.

☐

OPPOSITE

LAMB AND
NOODLE SOUP

─── SERVES 4 ───

PRAWN OMELETTES

*These light and tasty omelettes are flavoured with
garlic, shallot, chives and prawns.*

Step 4

Step 4

☐ 8 prawns, peeled   ☐ 1 tbsp oil   ☐ ½ tsp chopped garlic
☐ ½ tsp chopped shallot   ☐ 8 eggs, beaten   ☐ 4 tbsps chopped chives
☐ 4 tbsps oil   ☐ Salt and pepper

1. Cut the peeled prawns into small pieces.

2. Heat the 1 tbsp oil in a small frying pan and fry the prawns with the garlic and shallot until golden brown. Set aside.

3. Beat together the eggs and the chives. In a frying pan, cook several thin omelettes, using a little of the 4 tbsps oil for each one.

4. Cut rounds out of the cooked omelettes using a pastry cutter or a glass. Layer these rounds with the prawn filling.

5. Serve hot, either whole or cut into wedges.

☐ TIME   Preparation takes about 10 minutes and cooking takes approximately 20 minutes.

☐ SERVING IDEA   You could serve this dish cold with a tossed mixed salad.

☐ COOK'S TIP   The omelettes should be quite thin, like crepes.

☐

OPPOSITE

PRAWN
OMELETTES

SERVES 4

PEKING STYLE SOUP

*Duck stock is the base of this tasty, filling soup, which contains
meat and vegetables, the whole delicately flavoured with
sesame seeds and soy sauce.*

Step 1

Step 1

□ 4 slices smoked ham   □ 300g/12oz Chinese leaves   □ 700ml/1¼
pints duck stock   □ 1 tbsp sesame seeds   □ Pinch chopped garlic
□ 1 tbsp soy sauce   □ ½ tsp white wine vinegar
□ Salt and pepper   □ 1 egg yolk, beaten

1. Cut the ham into small, even-sized cubes.

2. Cut the Chinese leaves into small pieces and simmer briskly for 10
minutes in the duck stock.

3. Stir in the sesame seeds, garlic, ham, soy sauce, vinegar and salt and
pepper to taste.

4. Cook for 10 minutes over a gentle heat. Using a teaspoon, drizzle the
beaten egg yolk into the soup. Serve immediately.

□ TIME   Preparation takes about 5 minutes and cooking takes
approximately 20 minutes.

□ VARIATION   Replace the smoked ham with a different smoked
meat.

□ CHECKPOINT   The smoked ham is likely to change colour
during cooking.

□

OPPOSITE

PEKING STYLE
SOUP

---- SERVES 4 ----

FISH SOUP WITH SWEETCORN

*Home-made fish stock is the basis of a soup to which
corn and sliced, filleted fish are added.*

Step 1

Step 1

Step 1

☐ 1 tbsp oil   ☐ 1 carrot, chopped   ☐ 1 onion, chopped
☐ ½ leek, chopped   ☐ 1 bay leaf   ☐ 1kg/2¼lbs mixed fish
☐ 2 trout fillets   ☐ 1 cod or fresh haddock fillet ☐ 2 tbsps oyster sauce
☐ 1 tbsp soy sauce   ☐ ½ tsp cornflour, combined with a little water
☐ 225g/8oz canned sweetcorn   ☐ Salt and pepper

1. To make the fish stock, heat the oil in a large saucepan and gently fry the carrot, onion, leek and bay leaf. When the vegetables are nicely coloured, add the 1kg/2¼lbs mixed fish, together with all the heads and bones. Cover with water and boil for 30 minutes.

2. Strain through a fine sieve, reserving only the stock and discarding all the rest.

3. Slice the trout and cod or haddock fillets thinly crosswise and set them aside.

4. Measure 700ml/1¼ pints of fish stock into a saucepan and bring it to the boil.

5. Stir in the oyster sauce, soy sauce, cornflour and the corn.

6. Boil for 10 minutes, then turn off the heat and add the sliced fish.

7. Check the seasoning, adding salt and pepper as necessary. Allow to stand for 1 minute before serving.

☐ TIME   Preparation takes about 5 minutes, cooking, including cooking the stock, takes approximately 40 minutes.

☐ COOK'S TIP   To make the fish stock, use a mixture of the most economical varieties of fish, discarding nothing.

☐ WATCHPOINT   If the soup is still at boiling point when the fish is added at Step 6, it will be hot enough to cook the fish, providing this has been cut into thin slices.

☐

OPPOSITE

**FISH SOUP
WITH
SWEETCORN**

SERVES 4

IMPERIAL PORK ROLLS

These fried rice paper rolls are stuffed with a mixture of bean sprouts, black mushrooms and pork and served with a spicy fish sauce.

Step 4

Step 5

☐ ½ tbsp vinegar   ☐ 1 tbsp water   ☐ 1 tbsp fish sauce
☐ 1 tsp sugar   ☐ ½ tsp chopped fresh ginger root   ☐ Chilli sauce
☐ 4 dried Chinese black mushrooms, soaked for 15 minutes in warm water   ☐ 300g/12oz boned pork shoulder, very finely chopped   ☐ ½ tsp oil   ☐ 100g/4oz bean sprouts, blanched and drained   ☐ ½ tsp cornflour   ☐ 1 tbsp soy sauce   ☐ Salt and pepper
☐ 16 sheets rice paper, soaked in warm water for 10 minutes
☐ A little beaten egg   ☐ 100ml/4 fl oz oil

---

1. To make the sauce, mix together the vinegar, water, fish sauce, sugar and ginger and allow to stand for 30 minutes. Add a few drops of chilli sauce, just before serving.

2. Dice the mushrooms very finely and mix them with the meat.

3. Heat the ½ tsp oil in a wok and stir-fry the above together with the bean sprouts, soy sauce and cornflour for 2 minutes. Allow to cool. The mixture should be quite dry. Add salt, pepper and chilli sauce to taste.

4. Drain the rice paper sheets and spread them out on your work surface. Place a little of the cooled stuffing in the centre of each sheet, roll it up and seal the edges with a little of the beaten egg.

5. Heat the 100/4 fl oz oil in a wok and fry the rolls gently on all sides, beginning with the sealed side. Drain on kitchen paper.

6. Serve the rolls hot, with the sauce in individual bowls.

☐ TIME   Preparation takes about 30 minutes and cooking time is approximately 15 minutes.

☐ SERVING IDEA   Serve the rolls with lettuce leaves and fresh mint. Guests should wrap the mint and lettuce leaves around the rolls, before dipping them into the sauce.

☐

OPPOSITE

IMPERIAL PORK
ROLLS

---- SERVES 4 ----

NOODLES WITH GINGER
AND OYSTER SAUCE

*Noodles stir-fried with ginger, carrot and courgette,
then served in an oyster sauce.*

Step 3

Step 3

Step 3

□ 225g/8oz Chinese noodles   □ 1 carrot   □ 1 courgette
□ 3 slices fresh ginger root   □ 1 spring onion, cut into thin rounds
□ 1 tbsp oil   □ 1 tbsp soy sauce   □ 2 tbsps oyster sauce
□ Salt and pepper

1. Cook the noodles in boiling, salted water, rinse them under cold water, and set aside to drain.

2. Cut the carrot into thin strips. Thickly peel the courgette to include a little of the flesh and cut into thin strips. Discard the centre of the courgette.

3. Peel the fresh ginger root sparingly, but remove any hard parts. Cut into thin slices, using a potato peeler. Cut the slices into thin strips, using a very sharp knife. Heat the oil in a wok, and stir-fry the spring onion for 10 seconds; add the carrot, courgette and ginger, and stir-fry briefly.

4. Stir in the noodles and cook for 1 minute.

5. Stir in the soy and oyster sauces, and continue cooking until heated through. Season with salt and pepper and serve.

□ TIME   Preparation takes about 15 minutes and cooking takes approximately 15 minutes.

□ VARIATION   Cook the noodles in chicken stock instead of salted water to give them extra flavour.

□ CHECKPOINT   Stir-fry the ginger and the other vegetables very quickly, to avoid browning them. Lower the heat if necessary.

□

OPPOSITE

**NOODLES WITH
GINGER AND
OYSTER SAUCE**

———— SERVES 4 ————

RICE PAPER PARCELS
WITH ABALONE

Step 4

Step 5

Step 5

Step 6

□

OPPOSITE

RICE PAPER
PARCELS WITH
ABALONE

□ 12 sheets of rice paper, brushed with or dipped in warm water and then drained □ 225g/8oz canned abalone □ 4 tbsps oil □ ½ tsp each chopped fresh ginger root and garlic □ ½ spring onion, finely diced □ ¼ cucumber □ ½ green pepper, seeded and finely diced □ 225g/8oz fresh bean sprouts □ 1 tbsp soy sauce □ Salt and pepper

FOR THE SAUCE

□ 1 tbsp soy sauce □ 2 tsps wine vinegar □ ½ tsp sugar □ Salt and pepper

1. Cut 12 thin slices from the abalone. Cut the remaining abalone into small dice.

2. Heat 1 tbsp of the oil in a wok and stir-fry the garlic, ginger, diced abalone, spring onion, cucumber, pepper, bean sprouts and soy sauce for 5 minutes.

3. Remove from the wok and set aside to cool.

4. Spread out the rice paper sheets and divide the above stuffing evenly between them, placing it in the centre of each sheet.

5. Fold up first one side and then the other over the stuffing.

6. Next, fold in both ends to form 12 square parcels.

7. Heat 2 tbsps of the oil in a frying pan and gently cook the sliced abalone for a few minutes on both sides.

8. Heat the remaining oil and fry the rice paper parcels on both sides until golden brown. Drain on kitchen paper.

9. Mix together the sauce ingredients and serve the sauce in small individual bowls, to accompany the fried parcels and the sliced abalone.

□ TIME   Preparation takes about 25 minutes and cooking takes approximately 10 minutes.

□ SERVING IDEA   The parcels could be made larger or smaller as desired.

□ COOK'S TIP   Use square sheets of rice paper for this recipe, as they are much easier to fold up neatly than the round sheets.

——— SERVES 4 ———

STIR-FRIED RICE WITH PEPPERS

*Long grain rice stir-fried with red and green peppers,
onions and soy sauce.*

Step 2

Step 3

☐ 100g/4oz long grain rice   ☐ 1 tbsp peanut oil   ☐ 1 onion,
chopped   ☐ 1 green pepper, seeded and cut into small pieces
☐ 1 red pepper, seeded and cut into small pieces   ☐ 1 tbsp soy sauce
☐ Salt and pepper   ☐ 1 tsp sesame oil

1. Cook the rice in boiling water, drain and set aside.

2. Heat the oil in a wok and stir-fry the onion, add the peppers and fry until lightly browned.

3. Add the rice to the wok, stir in the soy sauce and continue cooking until the rice is heated through completely.

4. Season with salt, pepper and the sesame oil and serve.

☐ TIME   Preparation takes 5 minutes and cooking takes approximately 25 minutes.

☐ VARIATION   If you like the strong flavour of sesame oil, stir-fry the vegetables and rice in this instead of the peanut oil.

☐ CHECKPOINT   Do not overcook the rice in Step 1, or it will become sticky in Step 3.

☐

OPPOSITE

STIR-FRIED RICE
WITH PEPPERS

CELLOPHANE NOODLES WITH PRAWNS

*An oyster and wine sauce enhances this light
and tasty seafood dish.*

☐ 250g/9oz cellophane noodles   ☐ 1 spring onion   ☐ 1 tbsp oil
☐ 24 fresh prawns, peeled   ☐ 1 tbsp Chinese wine   ☐ 2 tbsps light
soy sauce   ☐ ½ tsp sugar   ☐ 1 tbsp oyster sauce   ☐ 50ml/2 fl oz
fish stock   ☐ Few drops sesame oil

Step 2

Step 2

Step 2

1. Cook the noodles in boiling, salted water for 1 minute. Drain and rinse under cold water. Set aside to drain.

2. To prepare the spring onion, slice off the roots and peel off the tough outer leaves before slicing the spring onion into thin rounds. Heat the oil in a wok and stir-fry the spring onion and the prawns for 1 minute.

3. Reduce the heat, drain off the excess fat, and deglaze the wok with the Chinese wine.

4. Stir in the drained noodles, soy sauce, sugar, oyster sauce, fish stock and sesame oil.

5. Cook until the noodles are heated through and then serve immediately.

☐ TIME   Preparation takes about 15 minutes and cooking takes approximately 15 minutes.

☐ VARIATION   The fresh prawns could be replaced with cooked ones.

☐ CHECKPOINT   When adding the noodles to the wok, the heat must be reduced considerably, or the noodles will be overcooked.

☐

OPPOSITE

CELLOPHANE
NOODLES WITH
PRAWNS

---- SERVES 4 ----

FRIED NOODLES WITH PORK AND VEGETABLES

Fried noodles, served with pork and vegetables in a rich, tasty sauce.

Step 1

Step 1

Step 1

□ 350g/12oz fresh noodles   □ 1 taro   □ 1 tbsp oil   □ 1 tsp chopped garlic   □ 1 carrot, cut into sticks   □ 225g/8oz Chinese leaves, sliced thinly   □ 225g/8oz cooked pork meat, sliced thinly   □ 1 tbsp soy sauce   □ 300ml/½ pint chicken stock   □ Salt and pepper   □ Oil for deep-frying   □ 1 tsp cornflour, combined with a little water

1. Cook the noodles in boiling, salted water, rinse in warm water and set aside to drain. Prepare the taro by first slicing off the end then peeling with a potato peeler. Lastly, using the potato peeler, cut the taro into thin slices.

2. Heat the oil in a wok and stir-fry the taro, garlic, carrot and Chinese leaves.

3. Add the pork, soy sauce, stock, and salt and pepper. Cook over a gentle heat for 5 minutes, shaking the wok frequently.

4. Heat the oil for deep-frying to 180°C/350°F and fry the noodles a few at a time. Drain the noodles on kitchen paper.

5. Share the noodles equally between four small plates.

6. Strain the vegetable and pork mixture from the wok and serve over the noodles.

7. Stir the cornflour into the remaining sauce in the wok, stirring until the sauce thickens. Pour some over each plate of noodles and serve immediately.

□ TIME   Preparation takes about 15 minutes and cooking takes approximately 25 minutes.

□ COOK'S TIP   As the noodles are fried, place them in an ovenproof dish in a warm oven, so that they will stay crisp while cooking the rest of the dish.

□ CHECKPOINT   Make sure the noodles are completely dry before cooking them in the oil, to avoid spattering.

□

OPPOSITE

FRIED NOODLES WITH PORK AND VEGETABLES

——— SERVES 4 ———

NOODLES WITH PEPPERS
AND GINGER

Chinese noodles with stir-fried peppers, ginger and garlic.

Step 2

Step 3

□ 1 red pepper, seeded   □ 1 green pepper, seeded   □ 225g/8oz Chinese noodles   □ 1 tbsp oil   □ 1 tsp each chopped fresh ginger root and garlic   □ Salt and pepper

1. Cut the peppers into six pieces.

2. Cut each of these pieces in half, to form slices.

3. Cut each slice into very thin matchsticks.

4. Cook the noodles in boiling, lightly salted water, stirring occasionally so that they do not stick.

5. Drain the noodles in a sieve and pass under cold running water. Set aside to drain.

6. Heat the oil in a wok and stir-fry the peppers, ginger and garlic for 1 minute, stirring continuously.

7. Add the well-drained noodles and stir-fry until the noodles are hot. Season to taste and serve immediately.

□ TIME   Preparation takes about 15 minutes, and cooking takes approximately 10 minutes.

□ VARIATION   If you have no fresh ginger root, substitute ground ginger.

□ CHECKPOINT   If the noodles stick together, run them under hot water until they separate, then drain off the water and continue with Step 7.

□

OPPOSITE

NOODLES WITH
PEPPERS AND
GINGER

STIR-FRIED STICKY RICE

*Glutinous rice cooked with stir-fried mushrooms,
ginger and shallots*

Step 4

Step 4

☐ 250g/9oz glutinous rice ☐ 2 tbsps oil ☐ 2 spring onions, chopped ☐ ½ onion, chopped ☐ 1 slice fresh ginger root ☐ 4 dried Chinese black mushrooms, soaked for 15 minutes in warm water, drained and sliced ☐ Salt and pepper

1. Wash the rice in plenty of cold water and place it in a sieve. Pour 1.3 litres/2¼ pints boiling water over the rice.

2. Heat the oil in a wok and fry the spring onions, onion and ginger until golden brown.

3. Add the mushrooms and continue cooking, stirring and shaking the wok frequently.

4. Add the rice and stir well. Pour over enough water to cover the rice by 1.25cm/½ inch.

5. Cover and cook over a moderate heat until there is almost no liquid left. Reduce the heat once again and continue cooking until all the liquid has been absorbed. This takes approximately 20 minutes in total.

6. Add salt and pepper to taste and serve immediately.

☐ TIME Preparation takes 5 minutes and cooking takes approximately 25 minutes.

☐ VARIATION Replace the water with beef stock to give the rice more flavour.

☐ CHECKPOINT Remove the ginger before serving the rice, as it is only used to flavour the dish.

☐

OPPOSITE

**STIR-FRIED
STICKY RICE**

CHOW MEIN

*Chinese noodles with pork and mushrooms, served
in a soy and chicken flavoured sauce.*

Step 3

Step 3

☐ 6 dried black Chinese mushrooms, soaked for 15 minutes in
warm water   ☐ 225g/8oz Chinese noodles   ☐ 150g/6oz bacon
☐ 1 tbsp oil   ☐ 1 onion, finely chopped   ☐ 1 tbsp soy sauce
☐ 50ml/2 fl oz chicken stock   ☐ Salt and pepper

---

1. Drain the mushrooms and slice them thinly.

2. Cook the noodles in boiling, salted water, rinse under cold water
and set aside to drain.

3. Cut the bacon into strips. Then cut the strips into small rectangular
pieces. Heat the oil in a wok and stir-fry the mushrooms, onion and
bacon for 1 minute.

4. Stir in the noodles, soy sauce, chicken stock, salt and pepper. Allow
to heat through completely and serve.

☐ TIME   Preparation takes about 5 minutes and cooking takes
approximately 15 minutes.

☐ VARIATION   There are many different shapes of Chinese noodles
and any of these can be used in this recipe.

☐

OPPOSITE

CHOW MEIN

—————— SERVES 4 ——————

FRIED NOODLES WITH PRAWNS

Deep-fried noodles served with a richly flavoured prawn sauce.

Step 6

☐ 200g/8oz fresh noodles   ☐ 2 tbsps oil   ☐ 1 red pepper, seeded and cut into small pieces   ☐ 1 tsp chopped garlic   ☐ 20 prawns, peeled and tails left on   ☐ 1 drop vinegar   ☐ 50ml/2 fl oz orange juice   ☐ ¼ tsp five-spice powder   ☐ 225ml/8 fl oz fish stock   ☐ 1 tsp cornflour, combined with a little water   ☐ Salt and pepper   ☐ Oil for deep-frying

---

1. Cook the noodles in boiling, salted water, then rinse in warm water, and set aside to drain.

2. Heat the oil in a wok and stir-fry the pepper and garlic.

3. Add the prawns and cook until crisp.

4. Stir in the vinegar, orange juice, five-spice powder and stock, and cook for 5 minutes.

5. Thicken the sauce by adding the cornflour and stirring continuously. Season with salt and pepper.

6. Heat the oil for deep-frying to 175°C/350°F, plunge in the noodles and fry them for 2 minutes, then drain them on kitchen paper.

7. Serve the noodles hot with the prawn sauce.

☐ TIME   Preparation takes about 20 minutes and cooking takes approximately 25 minutes.

☐ VARIATION   Any variety of noodle can be used for this recipe, but the long, thin type is best.

☐ CHECKPOINT   The noodles should be completely dry before plunging them into the hot oil to avoid spattering.

OPPOSITE

FRIED NOODLES
WITH PRAWNS

SERVES 4

STIR-FRIED TARO AND CARROTS

*Taro is a root vegetable which is like potatoes when small.
In this recipe it is cooked with carrots and flavoured with hoisin
sauce to make a delicious side dish.*

Step 1

Step 1

☐ 450g/1lb taro   ☐ 1 tbsp oil   ☐ 225g/8oz carrots, peeled and
cut into rounds   ☐ 2 tsps hoisin sauce   ☐ 100ml/4 fl oz beef stock
☐ Salt and pepper

1. Peel the taro and cut it into thin slices. Put the thin slices back in
place. Now cut the slices into thin strips. Heat the oil in a wok and stir-
fry the carrots and taro for 3 minutes, shaking the wok frequently.

2. Add the hoisin sauce and the stock and continue to cook until
slightly caramelized.

3. Season with salt and pepper and serve hot. The vegetables should
still be quite crisp.

☐ TIME   Preparation takes about 10 minutes and cooking takes
approximately 15-20 minutes.

☐ COOK'S TIP   When stir-frying the taro and carrots, give them
time to turn golden brown, before adding the hoisin sauce.

☐ VARIATION   If you cannot buy taro, use sweet potatoes instead.

☐

OPPOSITE

STIR-FRIED
TARO AND
CARROTS

CHINESE SALAD

*A lovely light, fresh salad, using lots of different vegetables.
Serve chilled with a sweet and sour sauce.*

Step 2

Step 2

□ 1 head lettuce, washed and dried   □ 4 slices ham, cut into
thin strips   □ 100g/4oz bamboo shoots   □ 225g/8oz bean sprouts,
blanched in boiling water and well drained   □ 1 carrot, cut into
thin strips   □ 3 palm hearts, cut in half lengthwise and then
in half again   □ ½ cucumber, cut into thin strips

FOR THE SAUCE

□ ½ tsp vinegar   □ 1 tbsp soy sauce   □ 1 tbsp oil   □ 1 tsp sugar
□ Salt and pepper

1. Shred the lettuce leaves finely and mix them with the ham. Arrange on a serving plate.

2. Prepare the bamboo shoots by slicing them first into long pieces, then cutting these pieces in half. Blanch the bamboo and drain. Sprinkle the bean sprouts over the lettuce and place the bamboo shoots over the top.

3. Garnish the salad with the other vegetables, making the dish look as attractive as possible.

4. Mix together the sauce ingredients and pour them over the prepared salad.

□ TIME   Preparation takes about 30 minutes.

□ VARIATION   Use any type of vegetable, prepared as above, to vary this salad.

□ COOK'S TIP   Cut the vegetables into very thin strips. This is important: as they are raw and therefore crunchy, some guests might have trouble with big chunks!

OPPOSITE

CHINESE SALAD

SERVES 4

CHICKEN AND BEAN SPROUT SALAD

*Steamed chicken and bean sprouts, coated in
a refreshingly light sauce.*

Step 2

Step 3

☐ 400g/14oz bean sprouts ☐ 300g/12oz chicken breast ☐ 1 tbsp soy sauce ☐ 2 tbsps chopped chives ☐ 1 tbsp white wine vinegar ☐ 1 tsp sugar ☐ 1 tbsp soy sauce ☐ Pinch chopped garlic ☐ 1 tbsp peanut oil ☐ ½ tsp sesame oil ☐ Salt and pepper

1. Cook the bean sprouts for 2 minutes in boiling water. Drain and refresh under cold water. Set aside to drain completely.

2. Sprinkle the chicken with 1 tsp soy sauce and cook in a Chinese steamer.

3. Once the chicken is cooked, set it aside to cool and then slice thinly.

4. Prepare the sauce by mixing together the remaining ingredients and seasoning with a little salt and pepper. Allow the sauce to stand for 20 minutes.

5. Mix together the bean sprouts and the chicken. Pour over the sauce and serve.

☐ TIME   Preparation takes about 15 minutes and cooking also takes about 15 minutes.

☐ VARIATION   The chicken could be cooked in stock, to which the soy sauce has been added.

☐ COOK'S TIP   Mix together the sauce ingredients the day before using them. The flavours will have more time to develop fully.

☐

OPPOSITE

CHICKEN AND
BEAN SPROUT
SALAD

STEAMED COURGETTE FLOWERS

*Try this if you can find courgettes with their flowers attached
– or if you grow your own. In this delicious recipe, they are stuffed,
steamed and served with a light sauce.*

Step 5

Step 6

☐ 450g/1lb boned pork shoulder ☐ ½ onion ☐ 1 tbsp oil
☐ ½ tsp chopped fresh ginger root ☐ 2 tbsps soy sauce
☐ 12 small courgettes with their flowers attached ☐ 1 drop
vinegar ☐ ½ tbsp sesame oil ☐ Salt and pepper

1. Cut the pork shoulder and the onion into very small cubes.

2. Heat the oil in a wok and stir-fry the ginger, pork and onion for
1 minute.

3. Stir in ½ tsp of the soy sauce and mix in well. Remove from the heat
and set aside.

4. Wash the courgettes and their flowers, then steam them for
30 seconds in a Chinese steamer.

5. Refresh by plunging into cold water. Open up the flowers, by
stretching them gently with your fingers.

6. Stuff the meat filling inside the flowers and down between the petals.
Close the flowers again by pulling the petals back into place, to form a
ball at the end of each courgette.

7. Put them back in the steamer and cook for 4 minutes.

8. Reheat the remaining meat stuffing.

9. Mix together the remaining soy sauce, the vinegar and sesame oil.
Pour this sauce over the courgettes and their flowers. Season with salt
and pepper, and serve with the reheated filling.

☐ TIME   Preparation takes about 30 minutes and cooking takes
approximately 20 minutes.

☐ VARIATION   As it is difficult to find courgettes with their flowers
intact, you can prepare this recipe using just courgettes, sliced into
rounds and steamed. Shape the rounds into 'roses' and place the
stuffing in the centre of each 'rose'.

☐ COOK'S TIP   You can stuff the flowers without presteaming
them, if the petals are already quite well opened.

☐

OPPOSITE

STEAMED
COURGETTE
FLOWERS

SERVES 4

STIR-FRIED CHINESE LEAVES

*Stir-fried Chinese leaves, courgettes and peppers,
flavoured with sesame oil and soy sauce.*

Step 1

Step 1

□ 450g/1lb Chinese leaves   □ 2 courgettes   □ 2 tbsps oil
□ 1 tsp chopped garlic   □ 1 tbsp chopped hot red pepper
□ 1 tbsp soy sauce   □ Salt and pepper   □ Few drops sesame oil

1. Shred the Chinese leaves quite finely. Prepare the courgettes, first topping and tailing them and then slicing down the sides, preserving a bit of the flesh with the peel. Slice finely. Heat the oil in a wok, add the Chinese leaves and garlic and stir-fry for 2 minutes.

2. Add the courgettes, hot red pepper, soy sauce, salt and pepper. Continue cooking for 3 minutes and serve hot with the sesame oil drizzled on top.

□ TIME   Preparation takes about 10 minutes and cooking takes approximately 5 minutes.

□ VARIATION   If you like hot, spicy dishes, add ¼ tsp of chilli sauce to the Chinese leaves.

□ SERVING IDEA   Cooked in this way, the Chinese leaves will remain crisp. If you prefer, cook them for longer for a softer texture.

□

OPPOSITE

**STIR-FRIED
CHINESE LEAVES**

STUFFED MANGE TOUT

*Steamed mange tout with a marvellous stir-fried stuffing of
abalone, spring onion and ginger.*

Step 2

Step 5

☐ 12 large mange tout   ☐ 1 tbsp oil   ☐ ½ tsp chopped fresh
ginger root   ☐ 1 spring onion, chopped   ☐ 4 pieces abalone, diced
☐ 1 tbsp soy sauce   ☐ Salt and pepper

FOR THE SAUCE

☐ 1 tbsp vinegar   ☐ 1 tsp sugar   ☐ 1 tbsp soy sauce
☐ 1 tbsp chopped fresh herbs

1. Blanch the mange tout in boiling, lightly salted water. Remove from
the water carefully and set aside to drain.

2. Cut the ends off each of the mange tout. Make an incision along one
side of each pod. Remove the small peas from inside and reserve.

3. Heat the oil in a wok and stir-fry the ginger, spring onion, abalone
and the small peas for 3 minutes.

4. Stir in the soy sauce and continue cooking until the soy sauce has
evaporated. Season with salt and pepper.

5. Fill each of the mangetout with the above stuffing and place them
side by side in a Chinese steamer.

6. Steam them until completely heated through.

7. Mix together the sauce ingredients and serve with the hot stuffed
mangetout.

☐ TIME   Preparation takes about 30 minutes and cooking takes
approximately 15 minutes.

☐ COOK'S TIP   To help prevent the stuffing falling out of the mange
tout, place them upright and side by side in the steamer.

☐ CHECKPOINT   Once the mange tout have been blanched, they
are quite fragile and should be handled with care.

☐

OPPOSITE

STUFFED
MANGE TOUT

—— SERVES 4 ——

BEAN SPROUT SALAD

*A marvellously light and refreshing salad, which can be
served as a starter to many Chinese meals.*

Step 3

Step 3

□ 400g/14oz fresh bean sprouts □ ½ red pepper, seeded
□ 1 carrot □ ½ cucumber □ 2 slices ham □ ½ tsp chopped
garlic □ ½ tsp chilli sauce □ 2 tbsps soy sauce □ Salt and
pepper □ 1 tbsp oil □ ½ tsp sugar □ 1 drop wine vinegar
□ 1 tbsp crushed tomato □ ½ tbsp sesame oil

1. Cook the bean sprouts in boiling water for 15 minutes. Refresh in
cold water and set aside to drain.

2. Cut the pepper, carrot, cucumber and ham into thin strips.

3. In a bowl, mix together the chopped garlic, chilli sauce, soy sauce,
salt, pepper, oil, sugar, vinegar and crushed tomato. Stir together well
to make a sauce.

4. Toss together the bean sprouts, vegetables and ham. Pour over the
sauce and the sesame oil. Serve chilled.

□ TIME   Preparation takes about 20 minutes and cooking takes
15 minutes.

□ SERVING IDEA   Sprinkle with freshly chopped chives.

□ COOK'S TIP   If you have not been able to buy fresh bean sprouts,
use the canned variety. Rinse them under cold running water and use
directly in the salad – there is no need to cook them.

□ VARIATION   You may prefer to use the bean sprouts either raw or
just lightly cooked.

□

OPPOSITE

BEAN SPROUT
SALAD

SERVES 4

CHINESE LEAF SALAD WITH MUSHROOMS

*Crisply-cooked Chinese leaves, served
in a stir-fried mushroom sauce.*

Step 2

Step 2

Step 2

□ 12 dried black Chinese mushrooms, soaked for 15 minutes in
warm water   □ ½ head Chinese leaves   □ 1 tbsp peanut oil
□ ½ clove garlic, chopped   □ 1 tbsp sugar   □ 2 tbsps soy sauce
□ ½ tbsp chopped parsley   □ Few drops sesame oil
□ Salt and pepper

---

1. Cook the mushrooms in boiling water for 15 minutes. Set aside to drain.

2. Prepare the Chinese leaves by separating the leaves from the heart, chopping each leaf into narrow strips. Blanch the Chinese leaves in boiling water for 1 minute. Refresh in cold water and leave to drain for 10 minutes.

3. Heat the oil in a wok and stir-fry the garlic, mushrooms and Chinese leaves for 2 minutes.

4. Stir the sugar, soy sauce and parsley into the wok and cook for a further 2 minutes.

5. Season with salt and pepper, drizzle over the sesame oil and serve immediately.

□ TIME   Preparation takes about 15 minutes and cooking takes approximately 20 minutes. The Chinese leaves must drain for 10 minutes.

□ VARIATION   If either the Chinese leaves or the Chinese mushrooms are not available, you could replace them with ordinary varieties.

□ CHECKPOINT   The cooking time for the mushrooms can vary considerably. If they are old, they will need cooking for slightly longer. Test from time to time, for flavour and texture, cooking until tender.

□

OPPOSITE

**CHINESE LEAF
SALAD WITH
MUSHROOMS**

—— SERVES 4 ——

VEGETABLE STIR-FRY

*A marvellous blend of Chinese vegetables and nuts, stir-fried in
a little oil and then cooked in an aromatic sauce.*

Step 1

Step 1

☐ 2 dried lotus roots, soaked overnight in water   ☐ 2 tbsps oil
☐ 150g/6oz bean sprouts   ☐ ½ red pepper, seeded and finely
chopped   ☐ ½ green pepper, seeded and finely chopped
☐ ½ spring onion, chopped   ☐ 300g/12oz Chinese leaves, finely
chopped   ☐ 1 cup dried Chinese black mushrooms, soaked for 1 hour
in warm water   ☐ 1 courgette, thinly sliced   ☐ 100g/4oz frozen peas
☐ 2 tbsps cashew nuts, roughly chopped   ☐ 1 tsp sugar
☐ 2 tbsps soy sauce   ☐ 400ml/¾ pint chicken stock
☐ Salt and pepper

1. Cook the lotus roots in boiling, lightly salted water for 20 minutes.
Slice thinly.

2. Heat the oil in a wok and stir-fry, in the following order, the bean
sprouts, peppers, onion, Chinese leaves, lotus root, mushrooms,
courgette, peas and cashew nuts.

3. Stir in the sugar, soy sauce and stock.

4. Season with salt and pepper and cook for 30 minutes, stirring
frequently.

5. Serve the vegetables slightly drained of the sauce.

☐ TIME   Preparation takes about 10 minutes and cooking takes
approximately 35 minutes.

☐ VARIATION   Any type of nut could be used in this recipe, for
example walnuts, hazelnuts or almonds.

☐ COOK'S TIP   If time permits, this recipe is even more delicious if
the vegetables are stir-fried separately, each cooked vegetable being
removed from the wok before continuing with the next. Finish by
cooking all the vegetables together for 30 minutes in the chicken stock
as above.

☐

OPPOSITE

VEGETABLE
STIR-FRY

—— SERVES 4 ——

MUSHROOM STEW

*Two types of mushrooms are cooked with oyster sauce and ginger
to make a delicious vegetable side dish.*

Step 2

Step 2

☐ 225g/8oz dried Chinese black mushrooms, soaked for 15 minutes in warm water   ☐ 225g/8oz dried Chinese mushrooms, soaked for 15 minutes in warm water   ☐ 1 tbsp oil   ☐ 1 tbsp each chopped garlic and fresh ginger root   ☐ 300ml/½ pint chicken stock   ☐ 1 tbsp oyster sauce   ☐ Salt and pepper

1. Cook the mushrooms in lightly boiling water for 45 minutes. Rinse under cold water and set aside to drain.

2. Heat the oil in a wok and stir-fry the garlic and ginger. Add the mushrooms and sauté briefly. Then add the stock, followed by the oyster sauce and salt and pepper to taste. Continue cooking until the sauce is thick and coats the mushrooms.

3. Serve hot.

☐ TIME   Preparation takes 10 minutes and cooking takes approximately 1 hour.

☐ SERVING IDEA   Just before serving, sprinkle over some freshly chopped parsley.

☐ CHECKPOINT   After removing the mushrooms from the cooking water, drain through a fine strainer, so that any sand or grit is trapped in the strainer and not on the mushrooms.

☐

OPPOSITE

MUSHROOM
STEW

———— SERVES 4 ————

CHINESE LEAF AND CUCUMBER SALAD

*Crisply-cooked Chinese leaves marinated with cucumber
in a slightly sweet sauce.*

Step 1

Step 1

Step 1

☐ 400g/14oz Chinese leaves, sliced thinly   ☐ 1 clove garlic   ☐ 1 tbsp soy sauce   ☐ 1 tsp sugar   ☐ 2 tbsps sesame oil   ☐ 400g/14oz cucumber, sliced thinly   ☐ Salt and pepper

1. Blanch the Chinese leaves in boiling, salted water for 1 minute. Set aside to drain. Prepare the garlic by first slicing the clove in half and removing the core. Then crush each half with the blade of a knife, and chop finely.

2. Mix together the garlic, soy sauce, sugar and sesame oil.

3. In a serving bowl, mix together the Chinese leaves and the cucumber and season with a little salt and pepper.

4. Pour over the marinade and leave at room temperature for 2 hours.

5. Serve at room temperature.

☐ TIME   Preparation takes about 20 minutes, cooking takes 1 minute and the salad needs 2 hours to marinate.

☐ CHECKPOINT   Do not make the mistake of overcooking the Chinese leaves, they should be blanched for 1 minute only, so they are tender but still crisp.

☐ VARIATION   Try using light or mushroom-flavoured soy sauce in this recipe.

☐

OPPOSITE

CHINESE LEAF
AND CUCUMBER
SALAD

VEGETABLE CHOP SUEY

*Stir-fried vegetables, simmered in a wok with chicken stock
and soy sauce.*

Step 1

Step 1

☐ 1 green pepper, seeded   ☐ 1 red pepper, seeded   ☐ 1 onion
☐ 1 carrot   ☐ ½ cucumber   ☐ 1 courgette, thickly peeled and
the central core discarded   ☐ 2 cloves garlic   ☐ 2 tbsps oil
☐ 2 tsps sugar   ☐ 2 tbsps soy sauce   ☐ 100ml/4 fl oz chicken stock
☐ Salt and pepper

1. Cut all the vegetables into thin slices. Prepare the onion by slicing it in half, then in quarters, and finally in thin, even slices.

2. Chop the garlic very finely.

3. Heat the oil in a wok and stir-fry the peppers and garlic for 30 seconds.

4. Add the onion and the carrot and stir-fry for a further 30 seconds.

5. Add the cucumber and the courgette, cook for a further 1 minute, stirring and shaking the wok continuously.

6. Stir in the sugar, soy sauce, chicken stock, salt and pepper, mixing together evenly. Simmer until all the ingredients are fully incorporated. Serve piping hot.

☐ TIME   Preparation takes about 15 minutes and cooking takes approximately 5 minutes.

☐ VARIATION   You could add blanched bean sprouts or sliced, blanched bamboo shoots to this dish.

☐ COOK'S TIP   If you follow the order given above for cooking the vegetables, they will all be cooked but still slightly crisp.

☐

OPPOSITE

VEGETABLE
CHOP SUEY

SCRAMBLED EGGS WITH CRAB MEAT

Fresh crab meat with richly flavoured scrambled eggs.

Step 3

Step 3

☐ 3 dried Chinese mushrooms, soaked for 15 minutes in warm water
☐ 1 carrot, chopped ☐ 1 leek, washed and chopped
☐ 1 onion, chopped ☐ 1 large crab ☐ 8 eggs, beaten
☐ Few drops sesame oil ☐ 1 tsp sake ☐ 1 tbsp soy sauce
☐ Salt and pepper

1. Cook the mushrooms in boiling, salted water for 15 minutes. Rinse in fresh water and set aside to drain.

2. Cook the crab for 15 minutes in a vegetable stock made from 2 litres/ 4 pints of water, the carrot, leek and onion. Remove the crab and set aside to cool.

3. When the crab is cool enough to handle, break off the pincers, break open the back and all the joints and remove the meat.

4. In a large bowl, mix together the eggs, sliced mushrooms, sesame oil, sake, soy sauce and the crab meat. Season with salt and pepper.

5. Cook by stirring the eggs over a very gentle heat in a nonstick frying pan. The eggs will thicken slowly. When cooked to your liking, serve immediately.

☐ TIME   Preparation takes about 30 minutes, as extracting the crab meat takes quite a while, and cooking takes approximately 30 minutes.

☐ TIMESAVER   The use of canned crab meat cuts the preparation and cooking time considerably.

☐ WATCHPOINT   Do not cook the eggs too quickly, or they will become hard and dry.

☐

OPPOSITE

SCRAMBLED EGGS WITH CRAB MEAT

SCRAMBLED EGGS
WITH PRAWNS

Fish-flavoured scrambled eggs, cooked with prawns.

Step 2

Step 2

□ 12 prawns, peeled   □ 8 eggs, beaten   □ ½ stick celery, cut into small dice   □ 1 spring onion, chopped   □ 1 tsp fish sauce   □ Salt and pepper

1. Cut the prawns into small pieces.

2. Stir the prawns into the eggs and add the celery, spring onion and fish sauce.

3. Season with a little salt and pepper.

4. Cook by stirring over a gentle heat. When cooked to your liking, serve immediately.

□ TIME   Preparation takes about 10 minutes and cooking takes approximately 10 minutes.

□ SERVING IDEA   Serve with lightly steamed prawns.

□ CHECKPOINT   The fish sauce is very salty. Only add more salt after cooking, if necessary.

□

OPPOSITE

SCRAMBLED
EGGS WITH
PRAWNS

—— SERVES 4 ——

BROCCOLI WITH OYSTERS

*Broccoli tips are cooked in a marvellous ginger sauce and
served with lightly poached oysters.*

Step 1

Step 1

□ 600g/1½lbs broccoli   □ 8 large oysters   □ 300ml/½ pint fish
stock   □ 1 tsp chopped fresh ginger root   □ 1 sprig fresh thyme
□ 1 tbsp oyster sauce   □ 1 tsp cornflour, combined with a little water
□ Salt and pepper

1. Choose fresh, green broccoli. Cut off the tough stalks, trim the
broccoli and rinse well. Precook the broccoli in boiling, lightly salted
water, until tender but still crisp. Refresh by plunging into cold water
and set aside to drain.

2. Open the oyster shells, cut out and set aside the oyster, discarding
both juice and shell.

3. Heat the fish stock and add the ginger, thyme and precooked
broccoli. Cook, covered, for 5 minutes.

4. Remove the broccoli and add the oysters in their place. Poach them
for 1 minute, then remove and place on a hot serving plate.

5. Stir the oyster sauce into the fish stock, remove the thyme and
thicken the sauce by stirring in the cornflour. Adjust the seasoning as
necessary.

6. Serve the oysters surrounded by the broccoli and accompanied by
the sauce.

□ TIME   Preparation takes about 15 minutes and cooking takes
approximately 25 minutes.

□ SERVING IDEA   If your guests are using chopsticks, serve the
sauce separately so guests can dip the oysters and the broccoli into it
using their own chopsticks.

□ COOK'S TIP   The sauce may be thick enough by itself without
using the cornflour, or it could be thickened by reduction.

□

OPPOSITE

BROCCOLI
WITH OYSTERS

―――― SERVES 4 ――――

CHINESE LEAVES WITH OYSTERS

Chinese leaves are here cooked in fish stock,
with oysters and bacon.

Step 1

Step 1

Step 1

☐ 12 large oysters   ☐ 450g/1lb Chinese leaves   ☐ 1 tbsp oil
☐ 225g/8oz bacon, diced   ☐ 4 tbsps fish stock   ☐ Salt and pepper

1. Use large oysters if possible. If you have to use the smaller variety, increase the number accordingly. Open the oysters, taking care to protect your hand by wrapping a tea towel around the oyster. Cut the oysters away from the shell, reserving the oysters and their juice, but discarding the shells.

2. Shred the Chinese leaves.

3. Heat the oil in a wok and stir-fry the bacon.

4. Stir the Chinese leaves into the wok and add the fish stock. Check the seasoning, adding salt and pepper to taste. Continue until the Chinese leaves are cooked to your liking.

5. Place the oysters and their juice on top of the Chinese leaves and poach for approximately 2 minutes.

6. Remove the oysters and place on a hot serving plate.

7. Serve immediately, accompanied with the cooked Chinese leaves.

☐ TIME   Preparation takes about 25 minutes and cooking takes approximately 10 minutes.

☐ CHECKPOINT   Taste the sauce before adding salt, as the bacon and oysters are naturally rather salty.

☐ COOK'S TIP   If you prefer your oysters a little more cooked, increase the cooking time by another 2 minutes. Do not overcook them, or they become chewy.

☐

OPPOSITE

CHINESE
LEAVES WITH
OYSTERS

——— SERVES 4 ———

FRIED CHINESE RAVIOLI
WITH SALMON

Wonton dough squares filled with a salmon stuffing and deep-fried.

Step 4

Step 5

Step 5

☐ 250g/9oz fresh salmon, boned, filleted and finely minced ☐ 1 tbsp chopped fresh chives ☐ 1 squeeze lemon juice ☐ 1 egg, beaten ☐ 24 wonton wrappers ☐ Salt and pepper ☐ Oil for deep-frying

1. Mix the salmon with the chives, lemon juice, salt and pepper.

2. Spread out 12 wonton wrappers and divide the stuffing evenly between them, placing it in the centre of each wrapper.

3. Brush the beaten egg around the edges of the stuffing and top with the remaining 12 wrappers.

4. Cut each one into the desired shape and seal the edges firmly by pinching with your fingers or pushing down with a fork. Set aside to rest for 15 minutes.

5. Heat the oil to 170°C/340°F. Cook the ravioli a few at a time in the hot oil. Remove when cooked and drain them on kitchen paper.

6. Season with salt and pepper and serve immediately.

☐ TIME Preparation takes about 20 minutes and cooking, depending on the number of batches, takes 8-15 minutes.

☐ SERVING IDEA Serve with slices of salmon, heated through in a frying pan, and chopped, fried onions.

☐ CHECKPOINT If you use a food processor to mince the fish, be careful not to reduce it to a purée; processing for a second or two is all that is necessary.

☐

OPPOSITE

**FRIED CHINESE
RAVIOLI WITH
SALMON**

SERVES 4

PRAWNS WITH VEGETABLES

Quick-fried prawns, served with stir-fried Chinese vegetables.

Step 1

Step 1

☐ ½ cucumber   ☐ 225g/8oz bean sprouts   ☐ 8 dried Chinese black mushrooms, soaked in warm water for 15 minutes   ☐ 2 tbsps peanut oil   ☐ 1 clove garlic, chopped   ☐ 1 tsp sugar   ☐ 1 tsp oyster sauce   ☐ 1 tsp wine vinegar   ☐ Salt and pepper   ☐ 1 tsp oil   ☐ 20 prawns, peeled and deveined·   ☐ 2 tbsps cornflour   ☐ 1 tbsp soy sauce   ☐ 1 tbsp sesame oil

1. Peel the cucumber all around with a sharp knife. Slice into julienne.

2. Rinse and drain the bean sprouts.

3. Drain the mushrooms and cook in boiling, salted water for 15 minutes. Rinse and set aside to drain.

4. Heat the peanut oil in a wok and stir-fry the garlic, bean sprouts and mushrooms for 1 minute.

5. Add the cucumber, sugar, oyster sauce, vinegar and salt and pepper, and cook for 2 minutes, stirring continuously.

6. Heat the oil in a frying pan. Toss the prawns in the cornflour and fry them until cooked through.

7. Transfer the vegetables to a serving platter. Top with the fried prawns. Sprinkle with soy sauce and the sesame oil just before serving.

☐ TIME   Preparation takes about 15-20 minutes, rehydrating the mushrooms 15 minutes and cooking takes approximately 10 minutes.

·☐ COOK'S TIP   It is advisable to devein the shrimp by removing the black thread from the indentation along the back of the prawn with a small, sharp knife.

☐ CHECKPOINT   Before serving, the vegetables should have caramelized slightly.

☐

OPPOSITE

PRAWNS WITH
VEGETABLES

PRAWNS WITH ONIONS

Diced onions are first marinated and then stir-fried with prawns and served in a soy-flavoured sauce.

Step 1

☐ 2 large onions, diced   ☐ 2 tbsps soy sauce   ☐ 2 tsps sugar
☐ 2 tbsps oil   ☐ 16 prawns, peeled and deveined   ☐ 100ml/4 fl oz
fish stock   ☐ Salt and pepper

1. Combine the diced onion with the soy sauce and the sugar. Marinate for 15 minutes, stirring frequently.

2. Heat the oil and stir-fry the prawns. Remove when cooked, but keep warm.

3. Add the onions and the marinade to the wok and stir-fry gently for 5 minutes. Season with salt and pepper to taste.

4. Add the stock to the onions, and continue cooking until the liquid has reduced. Serve the onions topped with the prawns.

☐ TIME   Preparation takes 10 minutes, marinating 15 minutes and cooking takes approximately 20 minutes.

☐ COOK'S TIP   Keep the fried prawns in a warm oven or reheat for 1 minute in a microwave oven before serving.

☐ CHECKPOINT   In Step 4, the liquid should be allowed to reduce considerably.

☐

OPPOSITE

PRAWNS WITH
ONIONS

SERVES 4

CRAB WITH BAMBOO SHOOTS

*Cooked crab, stir-fried with bamboo shoots and
served in a hot, spicy sauce.*

Step 1

Step 1

Step 1

□ 1 fresh chilli pepper   □ 2 medium-sized crabs, precooked for
approximately 15 minutes in fish stock   □ 225g/8oz bamboo shoots
□ 1 tbsp oil   □ 4 slices of fresh ginger root   □ ½ onion, chopped
□ 1 tsp vinegar   □ 1 tsp sugar   □ 200ml/8 fl oz fish stock
□ 1 tsp cornflour, blended with a little water   □ Salt and pepper
□ 1 tbsp chopped fresh chives

1. Prepare the fresh chilli pepper. Cut off the stalk end, slice the pepper in half and remove the pith and seeds from the centre. Chop the pepper as finely as possible.

2. Remove all the flesh from the cooked crab and set aside.

3. Cut the bamboo shoots into thin slices and blanch them in boiling, lightly salted water.

4. Heat the oil in a wok and stir-fry the ginger, onion and bamboo for 1 minute.

5. Stir in the crab and as much of the chilli pepper as you like, and fry for 1 minute.

6. Stir in the vinegar, sugar and fish stock and cook for 5 minutes over a gentle heat. Thicken by adding the cornflour, stirring continuously.

7. Season to taste with salt and pepper, sprinkle with chopped chives and serve.

□ TIME   Preparation takes about 20 minutes and cooking takes approximately 10 minutes.

□ VARIATION   If fresh crab is not available, use 2 medium-sized tins of crab, rinsed and well-drained.

□ CHECKPOINT   Add the fresh chilli pepper gradually, tasting after each addition to check the hotness of the dish.

□

OPPOSITE

CRAB WITH
BAMBOO SHOOTS

—— SERVES 4 ——

SWEET AND SOUR SHELLFISH

*Clams cooked in a light, sweet sauce and
served with matchstick vegetables.*

Step 2

Step 5

□ 20 clams, rinsed in plenty of running water   □ ½ cup Chinese wine
□ 1 tbsp oil   □ 1 tsp each finely chopped garlic and fresh ginger root
□ ½ red pepper, seeded and cut into thin matchsticks   □ ½ green
pepper, seeded and cut into thin matchsticks   □ ¼ cucumber, peeled
and cut into thin matchsticks   □ 1 tbsp soy sauce   □ 2 tbsps
pineapple or orange juice   □ 1 tsp wine vinegar   □ Salt and pepper

1. Place the clams in a wide-based saucepan, pour in the wine, cover,
and place over a high heat to open the shells, which should take
approximately 3-5 minutes.

2. Remove the clams from their shells. Drain the cooking liquid
through a very fine sieve and reserve. Keep the shells to one side.

3. Heat the oil in a wok and stir-fry the ginger, garlic, vegetables and
clams for 2 minutes.

4. Stir in the soy sauce, 4 tbsps of the reserved cooking liquid, the
pineapple or orange juice, and the vinegar. Season with salt and pepper
to taste. Cook until the sauce is slightly reduced and the clams are
tender.

5. Replace the cooked clams, with the sauce, in the reserved shells.
Cook in a hot oven for 2 minutes and serve immediately.

□ TIME   Preparation takes about 10 minutes and cooking takes
approximately 25 minutes.
□ VARIATION   Any shellfish could be used instead of the clams.
□ CHECKPOINT   Clams are often tough and rubbery and need to be
cooked long enough to tenderize them.

□

OPPOSITE

SWEET AND
SOUR SHELLFISH

—— SERVES 4 ——

SHELLFISH IN EGG
NOODLE NESTS

*Fried egg noodle nests are filled with mussels and cockles in an
oyster sauce and garnished with matchstick vegetables.*

Step 5

Step 5

Step 6

☐ 125g/5oz Chinese egg noodles   ☐ 24 mussels, washed and
thoroughly rinsed to remove sand   ☐ 150g/6oz cockles, washed and
thoroughly rinsed to remove sand   ☐ 200ml/8 fl oz Chinese wine
☐ 1 small courgette   ☐ Oil for deep-frying   ☐ 1 tbsp oil
☐ ½ tsp each finely chopped fresh ginger root and garlic
☐ 2 leaves Chinese cabbage, shredded   ☐ ½ tbsp soy sauce
☐ ½ tbsp oyster sauce   ☐ Salt and pepper

1. Cook the egg noodles in boiling, lightly salted water. Rinse under
cold water and set aside to drain.

2. Cook the mussels and cockles with the wine in a large covered
saucepan for about 3-5 minutes, until the shells have opened.

3. Remove the mussels and cockles from their shells.

4. Peel the courgette and slice the peel into thin matchsticks.
Discard the flesh and seeds.

5. Heat the oil in a deep-fat fryer to 180°C/350°F. Make the noodle nests
by placing a few noodles on the inside of a basket fryer or a metal
draining spoon. Clamp the noodles in place with a second basket or
draining spoon.

6. Plunge each nest into the hot oil and cook for 1-2 minutes until
golden brown and crisp. Remove the nest and drain it on kitchen
paper. Repeat the process with the remaining noodles.

7. Heat the 1 tbsp oil in a wok and stir-fry the garlic, ginger, cockles,
mussels and Chinese leaves for 1 minute.

8. Stir in the soy and oyster sauces and season to taste with salt and
pepper. Allow the liquid to reduce slightly. Divide the mixture evenly
between the fried egg noodle nests.

☐ TIME   Preparation takes about 40 minutes and cooking takes
approximately 50 minutes.

☐ SERVING IDEA   Serve on a bed of shredded lettuce.

☐ COOK'S TIP   Once the nests are cooked, tap the baskets or metal
spoons on a plate or table top to dislodge them.

☐

OPPOSITE

SHELLFISH IN
EGG NOODLE
NESTS

TROUT IN OYSTER SAUCE

*Steamed trout fillets served on a bed of vegetables
in sweet and sour sauce.*

Step 1

Step 1

Step 2

☐ 2 trout   ☐ 2 tbsps oyster sauce   ☐ 100g/4oz bamboo shoots, cut in matchsticks   ☐ 1 tbsp oil   ☐ 1 tsp each chopped fresh ginger root and garlic   ☐ ½ green pepper, finely chopped   ☐ ½ red pepper, finely chopped   ☐ ½ onion, finely chopped   ☐ 1 tsp sugar   ☐ 1 tsp vinegar   ☐ Juice of ½ orange   ☐ 2 tbsps soy sauce   ☐ 200ml/8 fl oz fish stock   ☐ 1 tsp cornflour, combined with a little water   ☐ Salt and pepper

1. Fillet the trout, then cut the fillets into several pieces.

2. Season the pieces with salt and pepper, and brush each one with oyster sauce. Then stack in pairs and set aside.

3. Blanch the bamboo shoots and rinse. Allow to drain.

4. Heat the oil in a wok and stir-fry the ginger, garlic, peppers, onion and bamboo shoots.

5. Add the sugar, vinegar, orange juice, soy sauce and fish stock and cook together for 3 minutes.

6. Season to taste, then add the cornflour, stirring continuously until thickened.

7. Steam the trout pieces separately for approximately 3 minutes, according to their thickness. Serve the fish on a bed of the vegetables in sauce.

☐ TIME   Preparation takes about 30 minutes and cooking takes 15 minutes.

☐ COOK'S TIP   Either freshwater or sea trout can be used in this dish, although sea trout is preferable.

☐ CHECKPOINT   The trout can be steamed whole and divided up just before serving. The cooking time should then be varied accordingly.

☐

OPPOSITE

TROUT IN
OYSTER SAUCE

SCALLOPS WITH ASPARAGUS

*Scallops accompanied with fresh asparagus and served with
a sweet and sour dipping sauce.*

Step 1

Step 1

Step 1

□ 16 scallops   □ 16 green asparagus spears   □ 1 tbsp oil

DIPPING SAUCE

□ 1 tbsp soy sauce   □ 2 tsps sugar   □ ½ spring onion, finely
chopped   □ 1 tbsp oil   □ 1 tsp wine vinegar   □ Salt and pepper

1. With the point of a sharp knife, pry open the scallops, and extract the scallop and the coral. Rinse well and allow to dry on a tea towel.

2. Boil the asparagus in salted water until tender, and refresh in cold water. Drain and halve lengthwise.

3. Make the dipping sauce, by combining the soy sauce, sugar, spring onion, oil, vinegar and salt and pepper to taste.

4. Brush the scallops and corals with oil and season with salt and pepper.

5. Preheat the grill or oil a frying pan, and quickly grill or sauté the scallops, turning them very gently. Cook for 1 minute on each side.

6. Serve the scallops with the asparagus to dip in the sauce.

□ TIME   Preparation takes 45 minutes and cooking takes 15 minutes.

□ COOK'S TIP   If possible, make the dipping sauce a day in advance, to allow the flavours to develop more fully.

□ CHECKPOINT   The grilling or frying of the scallops is a delicate operation which must be carried out quickly and gently, to avoid damaging the central body of the scallop.

□

OPPOSITE

SCALLOPS WITH
ASPARAGUS

SERVES 4

STIR-FRIED
LOBSTER WITH GINGER

Fresh lobster sautéed with courgettes in a pungent fish sauce.

Step 4

Step 5

□ 2 lobsters, each 350g/12oz in weight   □ 1 tbsp vinegar
□ 1 courgette   □ 1 tbsp oil   □ 2 tsps chopped fresh ginger root
□ 1 tbsp oyster sauce   □ 100ml/4 fl oz fish stock   □ 1 tsp cornflour,
combined with a little water   □ Salt and pepper

1. To cook the lobsters, bring a large pan of salted water to the boil, and add the vinegar. Drop in the lobsters and boil for 15 minutes. Drain, allow to cool and shell the lobsters.

2. Slice the lobster meat into serving-sized pieces.

3. Slice the courgette thinly.

4. In a wok, heat the oil, and stir-fry the ginger. Add the courgette and cook until tender but still crisp. Add the lobster and heat through.

5. Pour in the oyster sauce and the fish stock, season with salt and pepper to taste and allow to reduce.

6. Thicken the sauce with the cornflour paste, stirring continuously.

□ TIME   Preparation takes about 45 minutes, including cooking the lobsters, and cooking takes 15 minutes.

□ COOK'S TIP   Crawfish may be used instead of lobster.

□ CHECKPOINT   Use a nutcracker to break open the lobster claws.

□

OPPOSITE

STIR-FRIED
LOBSTER WITH
GINGER

—— SERVES 4 ——

CHINESE RAW FISH

Step 1

Step 2

□ 200g/½lb firm-fleshed fish fillets, e.g. haddock or cod   □ 200g/½lb sea bass   □ 1 tsp each finely chopped fresh ginger root and garlic   □ 1 tsp finely chopped shallot   □ Juice of 1 lemon   □ 10 coriander seeds, crushed   □ Few drops sesame oil   □ Salt and pepper   □ 1 tbsp chopped fresh chives

1. Slice the fish very thinly, spread the slices out on a plate, and sprinkle with the chopped ginger, garlic and shallot.

2. Squeeze on the lemon juice and sprinkle with the crushed coriander seeds.

3. Drizzle on the sesame oil.

4. Allow to marinate for 30 minutes.

5. Season with salt and pepper to taste, garnish with the chopped chives and serve.

□ TIME   Preparation takes about 45 minutes.

□ COOK'S TIP   Any fresh fish is suitable for this recipe.

□ CHECKPOINT   Do not allow the fish to marinate for more than 30 minutes, as it will become 'overcooked' by the acidity in the lemon juice.

□

OPPOSITE

CHINESE
RAW FISH

SERVES 4

BREAM IN SWEET
AND SOUR SAUCE

*Steamed fillet of sea bream, accompanied by
a spicy sweet and sour sauce.*

Step 1

Step 5

□ 1 sea bream, approximately 800g/1¾lbs □ ½ red pepper, seeded □ ½ green pepper, seeded □ ¼ cucumber □ 1 tbsp oil □ 1 tsp each finely chopped fresh ginger root and garlic □ 2 spring onions, finely chopped □ ¼ small fresh green chilli, seeded □ 3 tbsps pineapple juice □ 2 tbsps crushed tomato □ 150ml/5 fl oz fish stock □ 1 tsp cornflour, combined with a little water □ 1 tbsp vinegar □ Salt and pepper □ 1 sheet dried seaweed (optional) □ 1 tbsp chopped fresh chives

1. Scale and gut the bream. Fillet the fish, removing any bones, and cut the fillets into medium-sized pieces.

2. Cut the red and green peppers and the cucumber into fine julienne.

3. In a wok, heat the oil, and sauté for 1 minute the vegetables, ginger, garlic, spring onion and the ¼ chilli pepper. Add the pineapple juice, the crushed tomato and the fish stock. Simmer over a low heat for 2 minutes.

4. Thicken the sauce with the cornflour paste, stirring continuously. Discard the chilli pepper, add the vinegar and season with salt and pepper to taste.

5. Steam the bream over water containing strips of the dried seaweed, if using.

6. Serve the fish accompanied by the sweet and sour sauce and sprinkled with the chopped chives.

□ TIME Preparation takes about 30 minutes and cooking takes about 15 minutes.

□ COOK'S TIP Steaming the bream over water containing dried seaweed enhances the flavour of the fish.

□ CHECKPOINT As they cook, the pieces of bream will curl up.

□ BUYING GUIDE If you cannot obtain sea bream, substitute the same weight of red mullet.

□

OPPOSITE

BREAM IN
SWEET AND
SOUR SAUCE

SEA BASS IN FIVE-SPICE SAUCE

Fillets of sea bass are marinated and then quickly sautéed.

Step 1

Step 3

☐ 500g/1lb 2oz sea bass fillets ☐ 1 tbsp fish sauce ☐ 1 tbsp Shaohsing wine ☐ 1 tsp oyster sauce ☐ ½ tsp finely chopped fresh ginger root ☐ 2 shallots, chopped ☐ 2 tsps five-spice powder ☐ 1 tbsp oil ☐ Salt and pepper

1. Slice the sea bass fillets evenly. Arrange the slices on a plate.

2. In a bowl, combine the fish sauce, Shaohsing wine, oyster sauce, chopped ginger, shallots and five-spice powder.

3. Season the fish with salt and pepper and leave to marinate in the above mixture for 1 hour.

4. In a frying pan, heat the oil; drain the fish fillets and fry the fish briefly for 30 seconds on each side. Serve immediately.

☐ TIME   Preparation takes about 10 minutes, marinating takes 1 hour and cooking takes 1 minute.

☐ COOK'S TIP   The fish is generally served without a separate sauce, but if a sauce is preferred, mix together 1 tbsp fish sauce, 1 tbsp water, 1 tbsp soy sauce, 1 tsp sugar and ½ tsp five-spice powder.

☐

OPPOSITE

SEA BASS IN FIVE-SPICE SAUCE

—— SERVES 4 ——

BREADED PRAWNS WITH FRESH TOMATO SALAD

*Pan-fried, breaded prawns served with a fresh
tomato and ginger salad.*

Step 5

Step 5

☐ 5 ripe tomatoes   ☐ 1 tsp finely chopped fresh ginger root
☐ 1 tbsp finely chopped fresh chives   ☐ 24 fresh prawns
☐ 2 tbsps oil   ☐ 2 tbsps plain flour   ☐ 2 eggs, beaten   ☐ 4 tbsps
fine breadcrumbs   ☐ Salt and pepper

1. Bring a saucepan of water to the boil, and immerse the tomatoes in it for 15 seconds. Rinse immediately in cold water and allow to cool. Peel, seed and finely chop the tomatoes.

2. Mix the ginger and chives together thoroughly with the tomatoes. Season and allow to marinate for 2 hours in the refrigerator.

3. Shell the prawns, leaving the tails intact.

4. Heat the oil in a frying pan.

5. Dredge the prawns in the flour, then dip them in the beaten egg, and finally coat them in the breadcrumbs. Fry until golden.

6. Serve the fried prawns on a bed of chilled tomato salad, garnished with chopped chives, if desired.

☐ TIME   Preparation takes about 10 minutes, marinating takes 2 hours and cooking takes about 10 minutes.

☐ COOK'S TIP   Prepare the tomato salad a day in advance, so that the flavour of the ginger has time to develop fully.

☐

OPPOSITE

BREADED
PRAWNS WITH
FRESH TOMATO
SALAD

—— SERVES 4 ——

CRAB ROLLS

Chinese pancakes are first filled with a delicious crab mixture, then rolled up and quick-fried until crisp and golden.

Step 1

Step 1

Step 1

BATTER

☐ 75g/3oz plain flour, sieved ☐ Salt ☐ 4 eggs, beaten
☐ 100ml/4 fl oz water

FILLING

☐ 450g/1lb crab meat ☐ 1 egg, beaten ☐ 1 tbsp chopped spring onion
☐ 1 tbsp chopped fresh chives ☐ Salt and pepper ☐ 1 tsp soy sauce
☐ 50ml/2 fl oz oil ☐ 1 egg, beaten

1. Make the pancake batter first, by mixing together the flour, a large pinch of salt, the four eggs and the water. Beat the mixture well and set aside to rest for 10 minutes.

2. Mix together the crab meat, one single beaten egg, the spring onion, chives, salt and pepper to taste, and soy sauce.

3. Heat 1 tbsp of the oil in a wok and stir-fry the crab filling. Once cooked, remove the mixture from the wok and allow it to cool.

4. Use the batter to make pancakes. Cook them one at a time in a frying pan, using as little oil as necessary, until lightly browned on each side. Keep the cooked pancakes covered and warm while cooking the others.

5. Place a little of the crab mixture in the centre of each pancake. Roll them up as for spring rolls and use the one remaining egg to seal the ends and the sides. Set the rolls aside for a few minutes.

6. Heat the remaining oil in a frying pan and fry the rolls gently until crisp, then remove them from the oil, drain on kitchen paper and serve immediately.

☐ TIME   Preparation takes about 15 minutes and cooking takes approximately 30 minutes.

☐ SERVING IDEA   A tasty sauce to accompany these rolls can be made by mixing together 1 tbsp fish sauce, 100ml/4 fl oz fish stock, 2 tsps sugar and 1 tsp chopped fresh ginger root.

☐ COOK'S TIP   Cook the pancakes in a nonstick frying pan to avoid using oil. If using a traditional pan, use as little oil as necessary.

☐

OPPOSITE

CRAB ROLLS

————— SERVES 4 —————

TROUT FILLETS WITH GINGER AND SPRING ONION

Steamed trout fillets cooked with spring onion and ginger and served with a slightly sweet sauce.

Step 1

Step 1

☐ 4 sea trout fillets ☐ Salt and pepper ☐ 1 spring onion, chopped ☐ 1 tsp chopped fresh ginger root ☐ 100ml/4 fl oz vinegar ☐ 100ml/4 fl oz soy sauce ☐ 3 tsps sugar ☐ 100ml/4 fl oz fish stock

1. Season the trout fillets with salt and pepper. Lay them in a steam basket and sprinkle over the spring onion and the ginger. Set aside.

2. In a saucepan, mix together the vinegar, soy sauce, sugar and fish stock. Place over a high heat and allow to reduce and thicken.

3. While the sauce is cooking, steam the trout for about 5 minutes, until cooked.

4. Serve the fish fillets topped with the sauce.

☐ TIME Preparation takes about 5 minutes and cooking takes approximately 15 minutes.

☐ SERVING IDEA The vinegar sauce can be served hot or cold.

☐ CHECKPOINT Do not overcook the trout fillets. If they are quite thin, 3 minutes steaming may be sufficient.

☐

OPPOSITE

TROUT FILLETS WITH GINGER AND SPRING ONION

SERVES 4

MONKFISH WITH ONIONS AND VINEGAR SAUCE

Chunks of monkfish are cooked and served in an onion and vinegar sauce.

Step 1

Step 3

Step 3

□ 1 large monkfish, cleaned   □ 2 tbsps oil   □ 2 large onions, finely sliced   □ 2 tbsps white wine vinegar   □ 2 tsps sugar   □ 1 tbsp soy sauce   □ 300ml/12 fl oz fish stock   □ ½ tsp chopped fresh ginger root   □ Salt and pepper

1. Prepare the fish by pulling off the skin in one piece, easing the skin from around the head and then pulling it down gently, but firmly, towards the tail.

2. Cut off the the head and tail, and clean the inside thoroughly.

3. Fillet the fish by sliding a sharp knife between the flesh and the central bones on each side. Cut both fillets in half.

4. Heat the oil in a wok, stir-fry the onions gently until soft and then ease them up the sides of the wok.

5. Add the fish fillets to the wok, stir-fry for 1 minute, then push the onions back into the wok with the fish. Deglaze the pan with the vinegar and stir in the sugar, soy sauce, fish stock and ginger.

6. Season with salt and pepper to taste, stir well, cover and cook for 7 minutes over a gentle heat.

7. Remove the fish, cut it into thin slices and keep on a hot plate.

8. Add the cornflour to the sauce and stir continuously, until the sauce thickens.

9. Place the onions and their sauce on a hot serving plate. Place the sliced fish on top and serve immediately.

□ TIME   Preparation takes about 15 minutes and cooking takes approximately 15 minutes.

□ VARIATION   When spring onions are in season, use about five instead of the onions. They should be shredded finely and cooked as above.

□ CHECKPOINT   Cook the onions over a gentle heat, as they should be soft and transparent, not brown. Ease them up the sides of the wok as soon as they are cooked.

□

OPPOSITE

MONKFISH WITH ONIONS AND VINEGAR SAUCE

—— SERVES 4 ——

WHITING FRITTERS WITH COLD FISH SAUCE

Step 1

Step 2

□ 150g/6oz plain flour, sieved □ 1 tsp baking powder □ 100ml/
4 fl oz water □ 1 egg, beaten □ 1 tsp oil □ 450g/1lb
whiting fillets □ Salt and pepper □ Oil for deep-frying

SAUCE

□ 1 tbsp fish sauce □ 1 tbsp soy sauce □ 1 tbsp fish stock
□ Few leaves fresh mint, finely chopped

1. Make the batter by mixing together the sieved flour and the baking powder.

2. Mix in the water, followed by the egg.

3. Add the oil and a good pinch of salt and beat all the ingredients together well. Set the batter aside to rest for a few minutes.

4. Season the whiting fillets with salt and pepper and cut them into small strips.

5. Heat the oil for deep-frying. Dip the whiting strips into the batter and fry them in the hot oil until crisp and golden.

6. Remove the fritters and drain them on kitchen paper. Keep hot.

7. Meanwhile, mix together the sauce ingredients and serve with the hot whiting fritters.

□ TIME   Preparation takes about 15 minutes and cooking takes approximately 20 minutes, as you will need to fry the fritters in several batches.

□ VARIATION   If you do not have the sauce ingredients, the fritters are delicious with a little lemon juice.

□ COOK'S TIP   Make the sauce a few hours in advance. This gives the flavour of the mint time to develop.

□

OPPOSITE

WHITING
FRITTERS WITH
COLD FISH SAUCE

—— SERVES 4 ——

PORGY OR BREAM
WITH PINEAPPLE

*Steamed porgy or sea bream fillets, served with a
stir-fried pineapple sauce.*

Step 1

Step 1

□ 1 large porgy or sea bream   □ 2 tbsps oil   □ ½ tsp chopped garlic
□ 4 slices of canned pineapple, cut into small pieces
□ 1 tbsp soy sauce   □ 50ml/2 fl oz pineapple syrup, from the can
□ 300ml/10 fl oz fish stock   □ 1 tsp cornflour, combined with a little
water   □ Salt and pepper

1. Cut the fins off the fish. Fillet the fish, using a sharp knife to cut
between the flesh and the bones on each side. Discard the head, tail
and bones.

2. Heat 1 tbsp of the oil in a wok and stir-fry the garlic and the
pineapple pieces.

3. Pour off any excess fat and add the soy sauce, pineapple syrup and
fish stock. Allow the sauce to reduce a little and then add the cornflour,
stirring continuously, until the sauce thickens. Remove the sauce and
keep warm.

4. Heat the remaining oil in the cleaned wok and stir-fry the pieces of
fish, seasoning them with salt and pepper. Shake the wok frequently to
cook the fish evenly.

□ TIME   Preparation takes about 15 minutes and cooking takes
approximately 15 minutes.

□ VARIATION   You could vary this recipe by substituting the same
proportion of orange for the pineapple.

□ COOK'S TIP   Begin cooking the fish pieces skin side down and
allow them to become quite crisp before turning them to cook the
second side.

□ BUYING GUIDE   If you cannot obtain porgy or sea bream,
substitute red mullet.

□

OPPOSITE

PORGY OR
BREAM WITH
PINEAPPLE

SERVES 4

DEEP-FRIED 'STICKY' RICE
WITH PRAWNS

Fried glutinous rice with prawns, served in a sweet and sour sauce.

Step 6

Step 6

□ 200g/8oz glutinous rice   □ 20 large fresh prawns   □ 1 tbsp oil
□ 1 tsp finely chopped garlic   □ 1 tsp finely chopped fresh ginger root
□ 1 small green pepper, seeded and finely chopped   □ 1 small red
pepper, seeded and finely chopped   □ ½ cucumber, finely chopped
□ 1 onion, finely chopped   □ 1 tbsp soy sauce   □ Juice of 1 orange
□ ½ tbsp vinegar   □ 1 tsp sugar   □ 100ml/4 fl oz chicken stock
□ Oil for deep-frying   □ 1 tsp cornflour, combined with a little water
□ Salt and pepper

1. Steam the rice and allow to dry at room temperature.

2. Shell and devein the prawns.

3. In a frying pan, heat the oil, and briefly sauté first the ginger and garlic and then the prawns. Remove and set aside. Sauté the red and green peppers, onion and cucumber until cooked.

4. Add the soy sauce, orange juice, vinegar, sugar, chicken stock and salt and pepper to taste.

5. Return the prawns to the pan and cook over a low heat for approximately 10 minutes.

6. Meanwhile, heat the oil for deep-frying to 175°C/340°F. Form the glutinous rice into balls and fry until golden. Drain them on kitchen paper and place in a warm oven.

7. Thicken the prawns and sauce with the cornflour, and serve poured over the rice balls.

□ TIME   Preparation takes about 20 minutes and cooking takes about 15 minutes.

□ CHECKPOINT   The steaming and drying of glutinous rice is a lengthy process and should be done in advance.

□

OPPOSITE

DEEP-FRIED
'STICKY' RICE
WITH PRAWNS

---— SERVES 4 ——---

STEAMED PRAWNS

*Fresh prawns, garnished with courgette peel, steamed and
served with a fish flavoured sauce.*

☐ 1 tbsp fish sauce   ☐ 1 tbsp water   ☐ 1 tbsp wine vinegar
☐ 1 tbsp soy sauce   ☐ 2 tsps sugar   ☐ 10 fresh mint leaves, finely
chopped   ☐ 1 shallot, chopped   ☐ Salt and pepper   ☐ 12 fresh
prawns, peeled and cleaned   ☐ 2 medium-sized courgettes, peeled
and the peel cut into long strips

1. Mix together the fish sauce, water, vinegar, soy sauce, sugar, mint,
shallot and salt and pepper. Stir well and set aside for at least 1 hour.

2. Just before serving time, season the prawns with plenty of salt and
pepper.

3. Roll the strips of courgette peel around the prawns and cook them in
a Chinese steamer for 5 minutes.

4. Serve the prawns piping hot, accompanied with the sauce.

☐ TIME   Preparation takes about 20 minutes and cooking takes
about 10 minutes for 2 batches.

☐ COOK'S TIP   If the strips of courgette peel are not very pliable,
blanch them in boiling water for 30 seconds, before wrapping round
the prawns.

☐ COOK'S TIP   The sauce can be prepared just before cooking the
prawns, but it is much tastier if prepared at least 1 hour in advance.

Step 3

☐

OPPOSITE

STEAMED
PRAWNS

SEAFOOD CHOW MEIN

*Chinese noodles cooked with mussels, cockles and vegetables and
served in a rich ginger and wine flavoured sauce.*

Step 3

Step 4

□ 225g/8oz Chinese noodles □ ½ green pepper, seeded
□ ½ red pepper, seeded □ 1 tbsp oil □ ½ tsp chopped garlic
□ ½ tsp chopped fresh ginger root □ ½ spring onion, chopped
□ 150g/6oz uncooked mussels (shelled weight) □ 50g/2oz
uncooked cockles (shelled weight) □ 1 tbsp Chinese wine
□ 2 tbsps soy sauce □ Salt and pepper

1. Cook the noodles in boiling, salted water. Rinse them under cold
water and set aside to drain.

2. Cut the peppers into thin slices.

3. Heat the oil in a wok and stir-fry the garlic, ginger, peppers and
spring onion for 1 minute.

4. Stir in the mussels, cockles, Chinese wine, soy sauce and the cooked
noodles.

5. Mix together well, using chopsticks. Season with salt and pepper and
serve when cooked through completely.

□ TIME   Preparation takes about 15 minutes and cooking takes
approximately 15 minutes.

□ VARIATION   Add other types of seafood to this recipe.

□ CHECKPOINT   In Step 5 heat the noodles through thoroughly,
turning them in the sauce, to coat evenly.

□

OPPOSITE

SEAFOOD
CHOW MEIN

─── SERVES 4 ───

CHICKEN WITH LEMON SAUCE

*Quick-fried chicken served with dried Chinese black mushrooms
in a lemon and ginger sauce.*

Step 1

Step 2

□ 1 lemon, washed   □ 2 tbsps dried Chinese black mushrooms,
soaked for 15 minutes in warm water   □ 2 tbsps oil   □ 1 chicken,
boned and the meat cut into thin slices   □ 1 tsp chopped
fresh ginger root   □ 1 tsp wine vinegar   □ 1 tbsp soy sauce
□ 300ml/½ pint chicken stock   □ 1 tsp sugar   □ Salt and pepper

1. Peel the lemon with a potato peeler.

2. Cut the peel into thin julienne.

3. Blanch the julienne in boiling water and set aside to drain.

4. Squeeze and reserve the juice of the lemon.

5. Cook the reconstituted mushrooms in boiling, lightly salted water for 15 minutes and then rinse them in cold water. Drain the mushrooms thoroughly, and slice them thinly.

6. Heat the oil in a wok and stir-fry the chicken, ginger and lemon peel for 2 minutes.

7. Pour off any excess fat and deglaze the pan with the vinegar. Stir in the lemon juice, soy sauce, stock, sugar and mushrooms.

8. Reduce the heat and cook for 20 minutes. Season with salt and pepper to taste and serve hot.

□ TIME   Soaking the mushrooms takes 15 minutes, preparation takes about 25 minutes and cooking takes approximately 30 minutes.

□ SERVING IDEA   Serve with steamed or boiled rice.

□ COOK'S TIP   The lemon peel must be blanched before using, or it will give a bitter flavour to the dish.

□

OPPOSITE

CHICKEN WITH
LEMON SAUCE

STUFFED CHICKEN LEGS

For this appetising dish, chicken legs are stuffed and rolled, then steamed and served in a light ginger sauce.

Step 2

Step 3

Step 3

☐ 2 tbsps dried Chinese black mushrooms, soaked for 15 minutes in warm water ☐ 4 chicken legs, boned ☐ 1 egg, beaten ☐ ½ tsp finely chopped fresh ginger root ☐ 300ml/½ pint chicken stock ☐ ½ tsp sugar ☐ Salt and pepper ☐ 1 tsp cornflour, combined with a little water

1. Drain the mushrooms and cut them into thin slices.

2. Flatten out each piece of leg meat and brush a little beaten egg over the inside. Place the mushroom slices evenly over the 4 pieces of meat and sprinkle on half the ginger.

3. Roll up each piece of meat and secure with thin kitchen string. Steam the stuffed rolls for approximately 25 minutes, or until cooked.

4. Bring the stock to the boil and allow to reduce by half. Add the remaining ginger and the sugar and season with salt and pepper to taste.

5. Add the cornflour to the sauce, stirring continuously until the desired consistency is reached.

6. Serve the chicken rolls sliced into rounds and topped with the sauce.

☐ TIME   Soaking the mushrooms takes 15 minutes, preparation takes about 10 minutes and cooking takes approximately 30 minutes.

☐ VARIATION   Enrich the sauce with a few reconstituted Chinese mushrooms. Cut them into thin julienne and add to the sauce in Step 4.

☐ CHECKPOINT   The time required to cook the rolls will vary depending on their thickness; 25 minutes for thin rolls, slightly longer for thicker rolls.

☐

OPPOSITE

STUFFED
CHICKEN LEGS

——— SERVES 4 ———

CHICKEN BREASTS WITH SPRING ONION

Stuffed chicken breasts, steamed and served in a light soy-based sauce.

Step 2

Step 3

Step 4

□ 1 spring onion, cut into rounds   □ 1 carrot, cut into thin julienne
□ 1 tsp chopped garlic   □ 4 chicken breasts   □ Salt and pepper
□ 175ml/6 fl oz chicken stock   □ 1 tbsp soy sauce   □ ½ tsp sugar
□ 1 tsp cornflour, combined with a little water

1. Mix together the spring onion, carrot and half the garlic.

2. Slice the chicken breasts open lengthwise, without cutting through them completely.

3. Season the insides with salt and pepper and cover each breast with ¼ of the vegetable stuffing.

4. Pull the top half of the breast back into place. Season with salt and pepper. Steam for approximately 15 minutes until cooked through.

5. Bring the stock to the boil in a small saucepan. Stir in the soy sauce, sugar and the remaining garlic, simmer and allow to reduce for a few minutes.

6. Thicken the sauce by adding the dissolved cornflour and stirring continuously until the desired consistency is reached.

7. Cut the stuffed chicken breasts into slices and serve them topped with sauce.

□ TIME   Preparation takes about 10 minutes and cooking takes approximately 25 minutes.

□ SERVING IDEA   Serve with plain boiled or steamed rice, garnished with 1 tbsp chopped fresh chives.

□ CHECKPOINT   The spring onion and the carrot must be cut very thinly in order that they cook quickly during steaming.

□

OPPOSITE

CHICKEN
BREASTS WITH
SPRING ONION

—— SERVES 4 ——

CHICKEN WITH BAMBOO SHOOTS

*Quick-fried chicken and bamboo shoots, served in
a light ginger and oyster sauce.*

Step 1

Step 1

☐ 225g/8oz whole bamboo shoots or canned, sliced bamboo shoots   ☐ 1 tbsp sesame oil   ☐ 1 chicken, boned and the meat cut into thin slices   ☐ 1 tsp chopped garlic   ☐ ½ tsp chopped fresh ginger root   ☐ 1 tbsp Shaohsing wine   ☐ 1 tbsp oyster sauce   ☐ 300ml/½ pint chicken stock   ☐ Salt and pepper   ☐ 1 tsp cornflour, combined with a little water

---

1. Cut the bamboo shoots in half lengthwise and then cut into thin, half-moonshaped slices.

2. Blanch the slices of bamboo shoot in boiling water, drain and rinse in cold water. Set aside to drain thoroughly.

3. Heat the sesame oil in a wok and stir-fry the chicken, garlic and ginger.

4. Pour off any excess fat. Deglaze the wok with the wine.

5. Stir in the oyster sauce and the stock.

6. Add the bamboo shoots, season with salt and pepper and cook for 2 minutes.

7. Thicken the sauce by stirring in the cornflour and stirring continuously until the sauce reaches the desired consistency. Serve hot.

☐ TIME   Preparation takes about 20 minutes and cooking takes approximately 10 minutes.

☐ CHECKPOINT   Sesame oil gives a very strong flavour to this dish, so use half peanut oil and half sesame oil, if preferred.

<u>OPPOSITE</u>

**CHICKEN WITH
BAMBOO
SHOOTS**

---- SERVES 4 ----

BRAISED CHICKEN
WITH GINGER

*Boned chicken, coated with ginger and cooked in a vegetable and
ginger-flavoured stock.*

Step 5

Step 5

☐ 1 chicken, boned ☐ ½ tsp chopped fresh ginger root ☐ 1 carrot, cut into small cubes ☐ 1 turnip, cut into small cubes ☐ 1 courgette, cut into small cubes ☐ 1 onion, thinly sliced ☐ 5 slices fresh ginger root ☐ Salt and pepper

1. Separate the breast and the leg meat from the boned chicken. Keep each leg in one piece.

2. Place the remaining meat and the bones from the chicken in a saucepan, with just enough water to cover. Boil until the liquid has reduced to a quarter. Strain the stock through a fine sieve.

3. Sprinkle the chopped ginger on the inside of the 2 pieces of leg meat and season with salt and pepper. Roll up tightly and secure with kitchen string.

4. Add 150ml/¼ pint water to the stock and bring to the boil in a saucepan.

5. Add the prepared vegetables, sliced ginger, rolled leg meat and the 2 breasts. Cook for approximately 35 minutes or until the chicken is cooked through.

6. Take out the rolled leg meat, cut off the string and cut the meat into rounds. Spread the slices on a warmed serving plate.

7. Take out the chicken breasts and slice them thinly. Arrange the slices on the warmed plate with the leg meat. Remove the vegetables using a slotted spoon, arrange them around the meat and then pour over a little of the stock.

8. Serve piping hot.

☐ TIME Preparation takes about 20 minutes and cooking takes approximately 1 hour.

☐ VARIATION If you do not want to use the chicken for the stock, use a stock cube dissolved in water.

☐ COOK'S TIP If you are short of time, do not bone the legs, but simply cut slits in the meat and place the ginger in the slits.

☐
OPPOSITE

BRAISED
CHICKEN WITH
GINGER

CHICKEN WITH BEAN SPROUTS

*Marinated chicken, stir-fried with bean sprouts and served with
a sauce based on the marinade.*

Step 1

Step 2

☐ 1 chicken, boned ☐ 1 tbsp Chinese wine ☐ 1 tsp cornflour ☐ 225g/8oz bean sprouts ☐ 2 tbsps oil ☐ ½ spring onion, finely sliced ☐ 1 tsp sugar ☐ 300ml/½ pint chicken stock ☐ Salt and pepper

1. Bone the chicken and cut the meat into thin slices or strips.

2. Place the chicken on a plate and pour over the Chinese wine.

3. Sprinkle over the cornflour and stir together well. Leave to marinate for 30 minutes.

4. Blanch the bean sprouts in boiling, lightly salted water for 1 minute. Rinse under cold running water and set aside to drain.

5. Remove the chicken from the marinade with a spoon. Heat the oil in a wok and stir-fry the onions and the chicken.

6. Add the drained bean sprouts and the sugar. Stir in the marinade and the stock. Allow the chicken to cook through, which will take approximately 20 minutes. Check the seasoning, adding salt and pepper to taste. Serve immediately.

☐ TIME   Preparation takes about 20 minutes, marinating takes 30 minutes and cooking takes approximately 30 minutes.

☐ VARIATION   Use an ordinary onion if spring onion is not available.

☐ CHECKPOINT   As soon as you add the marinade to the wok, the mixture will thicken, so have the stock ready to pour in immediately and stir continuously until all the ingredients have been fully incorporated.

☐

OPPOSITE

CHICKEN WITH
BEAN SPROUTS

——— SERVES 4 ———

CHICKEN IN HOT PEPPER SAUCE

Stir-fried chicken served with peppers in a hot pepper sauce.

Step 1

Step 1

Step 1

□ 2 tbsps oil   □ 1 tsp chopped garlic   □ 1 chicken   □ 1 red pepper, seeded and cut into thin strips   □ 1 green pepper, seeded and cut into thin strips   □ 1 tsp wine vinegar   □ 1 tbsp light soy sauce   □ 1 tsp sugar   □ 300ml/½ pint chicken stock   □ 1 tbsp chilli sauce   □ Salt and pepper

1. First, bone the chicken. To bone the legs, cut down along the bone on all sides, drawing out the bone with an even movement. Cut all the chicken meat into thin strips. Heat the oil in a wok and stir-fry the garlic, chicken and the green and red peppers.

2. Pour off any excess oil and deglaze the wok with the vinegar. Stir in the soy sauce, sugar and stock.

3. Gradually stir in the chilli sauce, tasting after each addition. Season with a little salt and pepper to taste.

4. Cook until the sauce has reduced slightly. Serve piping hot.

□ TIME   Preparation takes about 10 minutes and cooking takes approximately 25 minutes.

□ VARIATION   A fresh green chilli pepper could be used instead of the chilli sauce. Seed it and chop very finely. Add sparingly to the wok and taste the sauce 1 minute after each addition: the flavour develops as the pepper is heated. Repeat the process to taste.

□ SERVING IDEA   Serve with plain boiled or steamed rice.

□

OPPOSITE

CHICKEN IN
HOT PEPPER
SAUCE

DUCK WITH MANGOES

*Oven-cooked duck breasts, served with sliced mango and
coated in a mango sauce.*

Step 1

Step 1

□ 2 ripe mangoes   □ 300ml/½ pint duck stock   □ 2 duck breasts
□ 1 tsp each finely chopped fresh ginger root and garlic
□ Salt and pepper   □ 2 tbsps oil   □ 1 tsp vinegar   □ 1 tbsp finely
chopped fresh chives

1. Peel the mangoes. Using a sharp knife, cut the flesh through to the
stone in several places all round each mango. Ease away the slices.

2. In a liquidiser, blend the slices from half a mango with the stock
until smooth.

3. Rub the duck breasts with the garlic and ginger and season with
salt and pepper. Heat the oil in a frying pan and seal the duck breasts
all over.

4. Remove the duck breasts from the frying pan and finish cooking in
a preheated, hot oven, 220°C/425°F/Gas Mark 7, for 15-20 minutes.

5. In a small saucepan, reduce the mango stock mixture with the
vinegar, adding salt and pepper to taste.

6. Heat the remaining mango slices in a steamer for 1 minute.

7. Slice the duck breasts and serve them with the hot mango slices
topped with the sauce. Sprinkle with the chives just before serving.

□ TIME   Preparation takes about 15 minutes and cooking takes
approximately 30 minutes.

□ COOK'S TIP   Cut the mangoes into thick slices, as they tend to
become rather fragile when heated.

□ MICROWAVE TIP   Place the slices of cold mango onto 4 plates
and heat them individually for 1 minute.

□

OPPOSITE

DUCK WITH
MANGOES

---- SERVES 4 ----

DUCKLING SALAD WITH SWEET AND SOUR SAUCE

A light, tasty salad to serve as a starter to a summer meal.

Step 5

□ 1 cooked duckling, cooled and boned □ ½ cucumber
□ 2 carrots □ 2 tbsps wine vinegar □ 1 tsp mustard
□ 1 tsp sugar □ 1 tbsp soy sauce □ ½ tbsp hoisin sauce
□ 1 tsp sesame oil □ 1 tbsp oil, preferably peanut
□ Salt and pepper

1. Cut the duckling meat into bite-sized chunks.

2. Cut the cucumber into thin slices.

3. Cut the carrots into thin julienne.

4. In a small bowl, whisk together the vinegar, mustard and sugar.

5. Add the soy sauce, followed by the hoisin sauce.

6. Lastly, whisk in the oils and season with salt and pepper to taste.

7. Divide the duckling meat and the vegetables evenly between 4 small plates, pour a little of the sauce over each portion and serve.

□ TIME   Preparation takes about 20 minutes.

□ CHECKPOINT   Do not overcook the duck, the meat for this salad should still be tender and juicy.

□ VARIATION   A variety of appropriate vegetables, such as bean sprouts, could be added.

□

OPPOSITE

DUCKLING SALAD
WITH SWEET
AND SOUR
SAUCE

DUCK WITH GINGER SAUCE

*Ginger-stuffed rolls of duck meat, stir-fried and served
in a delicious, smooth ginger sauce.*

Step 1

Step 1

□ 4 duck legs   □ 10 slices peeled fresh ginger root   □ 2 tbsps oil
□ 1 spring onion, chopped   □ 1 tsp chopped garlic   □ 1 tbsp soy sauce
□ 300ml/½ pint duck stock   □ 1 tsp cornflour, combined with a
little water   □ Salt and pepper

1. Chop off the ends of the duck legs and discard. Using a small sharp knife, slide the blade down the sides of the thigh bone and ease away all the meat. Cut the thigh meat into large slices. Cut the slices of ginger into fine julienne.

2. Place a little ginger on each slice of meat, roll up and secure with thin kitchen string.

3. Heat the oil in a wok and stir-fry the spring onion with the garlic. Add the duck rolls, together with any leftover duck meat and fry for 2 minutes.

4. Pour off any excess fat.

5. Stir in the soy sauce, any leftover ginger and the stock. Allow to cook through completely.

6. Thicken the sauce with the cornflour if desired. Check the seasoning, adding salt and pepper as necessary.

7. Cut off the string from each roll and serve hot, with the sauce.

□ TIME   Preparation takes about 25 minutes and cooking takes approximately 20 minutes.

□ VARIATION   If the ginger julienne are blanched before use, this gives a milder taste to the dish.

□ SERVING IDEA   If there is no time to assemble the rolls, simply stir-fry small pieces of duck with the ginger julienne and continue as before

□

OPPOSITE

DUCK WITH
GINGER SAUCE

SERVES 4

LACQUERED 'PEKING' DUCK

Duck breasts marinated in honey and soy sauce for 24 hours and baked in an ordinary oven.

Step 1

Step 3

□ ½ tsp soy sauce   □ 1 tbsp honey   □ 1 tsp five-spice powder
□ 1 tsp wine vinegar   □ 1 tsp chopped garlic   □ 1 tsp cornflour,
combined with a little water   □ 2 duck breasts   □ Salt and pepper

1. To make the marinade, mix together the soy sauce and the honey.

2. Sprinkle over the five-spice powder and stir in well.

3. Stir in the vinegar, garlic and cornflour.

4. Season the breasts with a little salt and pepper and place in an ovenproof dish. Pour the marinade over to coat the duck breasts entirely. Leave to marinate for 24 hours.

5. Cook the breasts in a hot oven, 220°C/425°F/Gas Mark 7, for approximately 20 minutes, basting frequently with the marinade.

6. To caramelize the tops, put under a hot grill for several minutes until crisp. Watch carefully to prevent them burning.

□ TIME   Marinating takes 24 hours, preparation takes about 5 minutes and cooking takes approximately 25 minutes.

□ COOK'S TIP   Start cooking the duck breasts skin side up, and turn them over during cooking. Turn again to glaze the skin side under a hot grill, before serving.

□ SERVING IDEA   To serve more people, make twice as much marinade and use a whole duck. Score the skin for the marinade to penetrate and cook the duck in the oven for about 45 minutes to 1 hour.

□

OPPOSITE

LACQUERED
'PEKING' DUCK

SERVES 4

DUCKLING IN FIVE-SPICE SAUCE

*Duckling slices cooked with water chestnuts, Chinese mushrooms
and bamboo shoots and served in a five-spice sauce.*

Step 1

Step 1

☐ 12 canned water chestnuts ☐ 100g/4oz bamboo shoots
☐ 1 tbsp sesame oil ☐ 1 tsp chopped fresh ginger root
☐ 1 duckling, boned and the meat cut into thin slices ☐ 4 dried
Chinese mushrooms, soaked in warm water for 15 minutes, drained
and chopped ☐ 300ml/½ pint duck stock ☐ 1 tsp five-spice
powder ☐ Salt and pepper ☐ 1 tsp cornflour, combined
with a little water

1. Rinse the water chestnuts and blanch in boiling, lightly salted water
for 10 minutes. Lift out and set them aside to drain.

2. Blanch the bamboo shoots in the same water, rinse and then drain.
Once well-drained, cut them into thin matchsticks.

3. Heat the sesame oil in a wok and stir-fry the ginger and the duckling
slices.

4. Remove the ginger and duckling with a slotted spoon and stir-fry the
bamboo shoots, chopped Chinese mushrooms and water chestnuts.

5. Pour off any excess fat and return the duckling and the ginger to the
wok with the previous ingredients. Add the duck stock and stir well.
Sprinkle over the five-spice powder and allow to cook for
approximately 15 minutes.

6. Check the seasoning, adding salt and pepper as necessary. Thicken
the sauce by stirring in the cornflour, stirring continuously until the
desired consistency is reached. Serve hot.

☐ TIME   Preparation takes about 25 minutes and cooking takes
approximately 30 minutes.

☐ VARIATION   If you have no duck stock, use chicken stock
instead. Duck breasts may be used instead of duckling.

☐ CHECKPOINT   The water chestnuts will remain very crunchy,
but they are not undercooked.

☐

OPPOSITE

DUCKLING IN
FIVE-SPICE
SAUCE

SERVES 4

DUCK WITH BAMBOO SHOOTS

*Stir-fried bamboo shoots, served with duck breasts and
a hoisin-based sauce.*

Step 3

Step 4

☐ 225g/8oz bamboo shoots, cut into thin slices   ☐ 75g/3oz sugar
☐ 150ml/5 fl oz water   ☐ 1 tsp chopped fresh ginger root
☐ 1 tbsp hoisin sauce   ☐ 2 duck breasts   ☐ 1 tbsp oil
☐ Salt and pepper

---

1. Cook the bamboo shoots in boiling, lightly salted water for
approximately 15 minutes. Drain thoroughly and set aside.

2. Mix the sugar and water together in a small saucepan, stirring
thoroughly.

3. Add the ginger and the hoisin sauce. Place over a gentle heat and
cook until a light syrup is formed.

4. Brush this syrup liberally over the duck breasts.

5. Heat the oil in a frying pan and add the duck breasts, skin-side down
first. Sear on each side. Take out and finish cooking in a hot oven,
220°C/425°F/Gas Mark 7, for approximately 15 minutes.

6. Shortly before the duck breasts are cooked, stir-fry the bamboo
shoots in the oil used to sear the duck breasts. Season with salt and
pepper and serve hot with the sliced duck breasts.

☐ TIME   Preparation takes about 10 minutes and total cooking time
is approximately 50 minutes.

☐ SERVING IDEA   Serve any leftover sauce in a small bowl to
accompany the duck.

☐ CHECKPOINT   Don't forget to begin searing the meat in the
frying pan skin-side down and then finish with the other side.

☐

OPPOSITE

DUCK WITH
BAMBOO SHOOTS

---— SERVES 4 ---—

DUCKLING WITH ONIONS

*Stir-fried onions and duckling, served in a rich sauce flavoured
with Chinese wine, soy sauce and hoisin sauce.*

Step 1

Step 2

□ 2 tbsps oil   □ 2 large onions, finely sliced   □ 1 duckling, boned
and the meat cut into slices   □ 2 tbsps Chinese wine   □ 1 tbsp soy
sauce   □ 1 tbsp hoisin sauce   □ 300ml/½ pint chicken stock
□ Salt and pepper

1. Heat the oil in a wok and stir-fry the onion until lightly browned.
Ease the onions up the side of the wok out of the oil, to keep them
warm.

2. Add the duckling to the wok and stir-fry until lightly browned.

3. Pour in the Chinese wine. Push the onions back into the bottom of
the wok, with the duckling.

4. Stir in the soy sauce, hoisin sauce and the stock. Allow to cook until
slightly reduced.

5. Season with salt and pepper and serve immediately.

□ TIME   Preparation takes about 15 minutes and cooking takes
approximately 15 minutes.

□ VARIATION   If duckling is not available, use duck breasts.

□

OPPOSITE

DUCKLING
WITH ONIONS

SERVES 4

DUCKLING WITH CASHEW NUTS

*Sliced duckling, cooked with fresh cashew nuts and served
in a slightly sweet sauce.*

Step 1

Step 1

☐ 10 fresh cashew nuts ☐ 2 tbsps oil ☐ ½ tsp chopped garlic
☐ 1 duckling, boned and the meat cut into slices ☐ 1 spring onion,
chopped ☐ 2 tbsps soy sauce ☐ 200ml/8 fl oz chicken stock
☐ ½ tsp vinegar ☐ 1 tsp sugar ☐ Salt and pepper

1. Shell the cashew nuts, using either the blunt side of a chopping knife
or a nutcracker. Remove the nuts from their shells and then slice into
thin strips, using a very sharp knife.

2. Heat the oil in a wok and stir-fry the garlic and duckling until the
meat is seared and browned.

3. Add the cashew nuts and the spring onion and stir-fry for 1 minute.
Pour off any excess fat.

4. Stir in the soy sauce, then the stock, vinegar and sugar. Season with
salt and pepper.

5. Continue cooking until the duckling is tender and the sauce has
reduced enough to coat the pieces of meat lightly.

☐ TIME   Preparation takes about 15 minutes and cooking takes
approximately 20 minutes.

☐ VARIATION   Use different nuts, such as brazil nuts, almonds or
hazelnuts. Duck breasts could be used instead of duckling.

**NB Step-by-step pictures show preparation of Brazil nuts, which may
be used as a substitute for cashew nuts in this dish.**

☐

OPPOSITE

DUCKLING
WITH CASHEW
NUTS

SERVES 4

DUCK WITH CORIANDER SAUCE

Duck stuffed with spring onion, bamboo shoots and Chinese mushrooms, served in a coriander flavoured sauce.

Step 2

Step 2

Step 3

Step 4

☐ 1 duck, boned, leg and breast meat reserved ☐ 1 spring onion
☐ 50g/2oz bamboo shoots, blanched ☐ 2 dried Chinese mushrooms, soaked for 15 minutes in warm water and drained
☐ 10 coriander seeds ☐ 300ml/½ pint duck stock
☐ 1 tsp cornflour, combined with a little water ☐ Salt and pepper

---

1. Skin the duck breasts and reserve both meat and skin.

2. In a food processor process each of the following ingredients separately. One duck breast should be finely processed and then the spring onion, the bamboo shoots and the Chinese mushrooms should all be lightly processed. Mix all the processed ingredients together in a small bowl.

3. Spread this stuffing mixture onto the boned leg meat and the remaining breast.

4. Roll the meat around the stuffing and wrap each one in cling film. Twist the ends to seal well.

5. Steam the duck rolls in a steamer for 35 minutes.

6. Crush the coriander seeds and put into a small saucepan. Add the duck stock and cook over a gentle heat until reduced by a quarter. Thicken, if necessary, with the cornflour, stirring continuously until the desired consistency is reached. Season to taste with salt and pepper.

7. Heat the oil in a frying pan and fry the reserved duck skin until crisp. Leave to cool and then cut into small pieces.

8. Remove the cling film from the duck. Serve the rolls sliced into rounds, with some of the crispy skin pieces and the sauce.

☐ TIME Preparation takes about 30 minutes and cooking takes approximately 50 minutes.

☐ PREPARATION Either cook the remaining duck meat at the same time as you steam the rolls or keep it for another dish.

☐ VARIATION If available, add some chopped fresh coriander to the sauce.

☐

OPPOSITE

DUCK WITH CORIANDER SAUCE

CARAMELIZED SPARERIBS

These sweet, caramelized spareribs are always a success.
Tell guests to use their fingers; knives or chopsticks are out of the question.

Step 2

Step 3

☐ 1 carrot ☐ 1 leek ☐ 1 bay leaf ☐ 900g/2lbs pork spareribs, separated ☐ 1 tbsp honey ☐ 1 tbsp white wine vinegar ☐ 1 tsp chopped garlic ☐ 2 tbsps soy sauce ☐ 50ml/2 fl oz chicken stock ☐ Salt and pepper

1. In a large saucepan combine 2 litres/3¾ pints of water with the carrot, bay leaf and leek. Bring to the boil and add the spareribs. Blanch the meat for 10 minutes, remove from the stock and drain well.

2. Lay the ribs in an ovenproof dish. Combine the honey, vinegar and garlic, and spread the mixture on the ribs.

3. Add the soy sauce and the stock to the dish. Season well with salt and pepper.

4. Put into a very hot oven, 240°C/475°F/Gas Mark 9, and cook until the ribs are caramelized and have turned a rich, dark brown colour.

☐ TIME Preparation takes about 5 minutes and cooking takes approximately 55 minutes, from start to finish.

☐ SERVING IDEA Serve on a bed of finely shredded lettuce leaves, lightly seasoned with salt and pepper.

☐

OPPOSITE

CARAMELIZED
SPARERIBS

RICE-COATED MEATBALLS

*These highly seasoned meatballs, coated in pre-soaked rice, could
also be made using any type of meat.*

Step 1

Step 2

□ 100g/4oz long grain rice, pre-soaked in warm water for 2 hours
□ 600g/1lb 6oz boned pork shoulder, minced □ 1-inch piece fresh
ginger root, peeled and chopped □ ½ tsp shallots, finely chopped
□ ½ tsp finely chopped fresh parsley □ ½ tsp finely chopped
fresh chives □ ½ tsp soy sauce □ ½ egg, beaten □ Tip of a knife
of chilli sauce □ Salt and pepper

1. Mix together the meat, ginger, shallots, parsley, chives, soy sauce, egg and chilli sauce. Beat well to combine all the ingredients.

2. Season with salt and pepper and then form into small meat balls.

3. Drain the rice very carefully, shaking well to remove all the water. Spread the rice on your work surface.

4. Roll the meat balls in the rice to coat them evenly.

5. Steam the meat balls for approximately 15 minutes. The exact cooking time will depend on the thickness of your meatballs, but small ones take 15 minutes.

□ TIME   Pre-soaking the rice takes 2 hours, preparation takes about 30 minutes and cooking takes approximately 15-20 minutes if you can steam all the meat balls in one batch, longer if you need to do two batches.

□ COOK'S TIP   Rinse your hands in cold water before shaping the meat balls, otherwise they tend to stick and break up.

□ VARIATION   Any type of meat can be used for these meat balls, so try beef, veal or even chicken.

□

OPPOSITE

RICE-COATED
MEATBALLS

SERVES 4

PORK IN SWEET AND SOUR SAUCE

Pork with matchstick vegetables in a marvellous sweet and sour sauce.

Step 5

Step 5

☐ 1 onion   ☐ ¼ cucumber   ☐ ½ red pepper, seeded   ☐ ½ green pepper, seeded   ☐ 1 slice pineapple, fresh or canned   ☐ 4 tbsps pineapple juice   ☐ 3 tbsps wine vinegar   ☐ 1 tsp chilli sauce   ☐ 1 tbsp sugar   ☐ ½ tomato, peeled, seeded and crushed   ☐ 300ml/12 fl oz   ☐ Salt and pepper chicken stock   ☐ 2 tbsps oil   ☐ 450g/1lb pork, cut into thin strips   ☐ 1 clove garlic, chopped   ☐ 1 tsp cornflour, mixed with 1 tsp water   ☐ Salt and pepper

1. Cut the onion, cucumber, red and green pepper and pineapple into thin matchsticks.

2. In a small bowl, mix together the pineapple juice, vinegar, chilli sauce, sugar, crushed tomato and chicken stock.

3. Heat the oil in a wok, stir-fry the pork and the garlic. Once the meat is golden brown, remove with a slotted spoon and set aside.

4. Add all the vegetables and the pineapple to the wok and stir-fry for 2 minutes.

5. Return the pork to the wok with the vegetables and pineapple and pour over the contents of the bowl. Cook for 3-4 minutes, stirring, and shaking the wok from time to time.

6. Thicken the sauce by adding the cornflour gradually, stirring continuously until the desired consistency is reached. Season to taste with salt and pepper.

7. Serve piping hot.

☐ TIME   Preparation takes about 25 minutes and cooking takes approximately 40 minutes.

☐ VARIATION   Replace the pineapple juice with orange juice.

☐ CHECKPOINT   The vegetables must be stir-fried quickly so that they remain slightly crisp.

☐

OPPOSITE

PORK IN SWEET AND SOUR SAUCE

— SERVES 4 —

PORK SLICES WITH
CRUNCHY VEGETABLES

*This dish has a cold sauce to accompany lightly steamed vegetables
and thinly sliced pork.*

Step 4

Step 4

□ 1 tbsp light soy sauce   □ 1 tbsp Chinese wine   □ 1 tsp sugar
□ 1-inch piece of fresh ginger root, peeled and finely chopped
□ 450g/1lb lean pork   □ Salt and pepper   □ 1 carrot
□ 1 stick celery   □ ½ fennel bulb

1. For the sauce, mix together the soy sauce, Chinese wine, sugar and
ginger in a small bowl. Allow to stand for 30 minutes for the flavours to
develop before serving.

2. Cut the pork into very thin slices and season with salt and pepper.

3. Cut the carrot, celery and fennel into thin julienne. Place them in a
steaming basket and steam for 3 minutes.

4. Remove the basket from the steamer and lay the slices of pork over
the vegetables. Return the basket to the steamer and cook for another
5 minutes.

5. Serve the steamed pork and vegetables accompanied with the cold
sauce.

□ TIME   The sauce must stand for 30 minutes, preparation takes
about 15 minutes and cooking takes approximately 8-10 minutes.

□ VARIATION   You can use any vegetables for this recipe.

□ CHECKPOINT   Carrots take longer to cook than celery and
should therefore be cut into thinner strips to ensure even cooking.

OPPOSITE

PORK SLICES
WITH CRUNCHY
VEGETABLES

STIR-FRIED PORK AND VEGETABLES

A quick and easy stir-fry of pork, bean sprouts and carrot, served in a spicy, slightly sweet sauce.

Step 4

Step 5

☐ 1 carrot, cut into thin matchsticks   ☐ 225g/8oz bean sprouts   ☐ 2 tbsps oil   ☐ Slice of fresh ginger root   ☐ 1 spring onion, chopped   ☐ ½ tsp chopped garlic   ☐ 450g/1lb pork, cut into thin slices   ☐ 2 tsps sake   ☐ 300ml/½ pint chicken stock   ☐ Salt and pepper   ☐ ½ tsp brown sugar   ☐ 1 tsp cornflour, combined with a little water

1. In a small saucepan, bring to the boil a little salted water. Blanch the julienned carrot in this water for 1 minute. Drain well, reserving the water.

2. Wash the bean sprouts in lots of running water and blanch for 1 minute in the water used for the carrot. Rinse well and drain.

3. Heat the oil in a wok. Stir-fry the ginger, spring onion and the garlic until slightly coloured.

4. Add the meat, stir in well and cook for 1 minute.

5. Add the well-drained vegetables, wine and stock. Season with salt and pepper, stir together well and cook for 2 minutes.

6. Using a slotted spoon, take out the meat and the vegetables, and keep warm.

7. Add the sugar to the contents of the wok and thicken the sauce with the cornflour, adding it gradually and stirring continuously until the desired consistency is reached.

8. Remove the ginger, return the meat and vegetables to the wok and serve hot.

☐ TIME   Preparation takes about 25 minutes and cooking takes approximately 10 minutes.

☐ SERVING IDEA   Sprinkle a few drops of sesame oil over the finished dish.

☐ COOK'S TIP   Stir-fry the spring onion and the ginger before the chopped garlic, as the garlic tends to stick and brown before the spring onion is cooked.

☐

OPPOSITE

STIR-FRIED PORK AND VEGETABLES

PORK WITH GREEN PEPPERS

A quickly-prepared stir-fried pork dish with green peppers and a hoisin-based sauce.

Step 1

□ 450g/1lb pork fillet   □ 2 tbsps oil   □ ½ tsp chopped garlic
□ 2 green peppers, seeded and cut into thin matchsticks   □ 1 tsp wine
vinegar   □ 2 tbsps chicken stock   □ 1 tbsp hoisin sauce
□ Salt and pepper   □ 1 tsp cornflour, combined with a little water

1. Slice the pork thinly, then cut into narrow strips. Heat the oil in a wok. Add the garlic, green pepper and the meat. Stir together well. Cook for 1 minute, shaking the wok occasionally.

2. Stir in the vinegar, stock and hoisin sauce. Season to taste with salt and pepper. Cook for 3 minutes.

3. Stir in the cornflour and cook, stirring continuously, until the desired consistency is reached.

□ TIME   Preparation takes about 10 minutes and cooking takes 5 minutes.

□ VARIATION   Replace the green pepper with a red one.

□ CHECKPOINT   It is not necessary to add sugar to this sauce, as the hoisin sauce is sweet enough.

□

OPPOSITE

PORK WITH
GREEN PEPPERS

—— SERVES 4 ——

PORK SPARERIBS WITH CHINESE MUSHROOMS

Spareribs served with Chinese mushrooms in a slightly hot and spicy sauce.

Step 1

Step 1

Step 1

□ 900g/2lbs pork spareribs   □ 1 carrot, finely sliced   □ 1 leek, finely chopped   □ 1 bay leaf   □ 150g/6oz dried Chinese mushrooms, soaked for 15 minutes in warm water and drained   □ 1 tbsp oil   □ 1 tsp chopped garlic   □ ½ tsp chilli sauce   □ 1 tbsp soy sauce   □ 1 tbsp hoisin sauce   □ 1 tsp wine vinegar   □ 300ml/½ pint chicken stock   □ Salt and pepper

1. Cut the spareribs down the bone to separate them. Now cut them into smaller pieces, so that they are easier to handle. In a medium-sized, flameproof casserole bring to the boil plenty of water to which you have added the carrot, leek and bay leaf. Blanch the spareribs for 1 minute in the boiling water. Drain well.

2. Cook the mushrooms in the boiling water for 10 minutes. Drain well.

3. Heat the oil in a wok, add the garlic, chilli sauce and the mushrooms. Fry slowly until lightly coloured.

4. Stir in the soy sauce, hoisin sauce, vinegar and stock.

5. Add the spareribs, stirring all the ingredients together well. Season with salt and pepper to taste and cook, covered, for 10 minutes.

6. Remove the lid and allow the sauce to reduce slightly. Serve piping hot.

□ TIME   Preparation takes about 15 minutes, soaking the mushrooms about 15 minutes and cooking takes approximately 20 minutes.

□ VARIATION   If you cannot buy hoisin sauce, replace it with 1 tsp sugar.

□ CHECKPOINT   You should not blanch the spareribs for longer than 1 minute.

□

OPPOSITE

PORK SPARERIBS WITH CHINESE MUSHROOMS

—— SERVES 4 ——

CARAMELIZED PORK

Paper thin slices of pork fillet cooked and served in a slightly sweet caramel sauce.

Step 3

Step 4

☐ 2 tbsps dark soy sauce ☐ 1 tbsp Shaohsing wine ☐ 1 tbsp hoisin sauce ☐ 1 tsp honey ☐ Few drops chilli sauce ☐ ½ tbsp oil ☐ 450g/1lb pork fillet ☐ Salt and pepper

1. In a small bowl, mix together the soy sauce, Shaohsing wine, hoisin sauce, honey, chilli sauce and the oil. Stir together well.

2. Cut off any excess fat from the pork fillet and remove any gristle and nerves.

3. Roll the fillet up and secure with thin kitchen string. Place the fillet in an ovenproof dish.

4. Pour over the prepared sauce and cook in a moderate oven, 180°C/350°F/Gas mark 4. Baste the roast with the sauce during cooking, so that it builds up in caramelized layers around the meat. The pork should be roasted until cooked through completely, which should take approximately 30 minutes.

5. Remove the roast from the oven and place the meat on a cutting board. Pour any remaining sauce into a sauce boat.

6. Cut the meat into paper thin slices and arrange on a warmed serving plate. Serve immediately with the remaining sauce.

☐ TIME   Preparation takes about 15 minutes and cooking takes approximately 30 minutes.

☐ SERVING IDEA   This dish can also be served cold with a mixed green side salad.

☐ CHECKPOINT   Should the bottom of the ovenproof dish start to burn during cooking, add a little water or stock.

☐

OPPOSITE

CARAMELIZED
PORK

—— SERVES 4 ——

PORK WITH BAMBOO SHOOTS

Stir-fried pork, served with bamboo shoots and courgettes.

Step 5

Step 5

□ 450g/1lb lean pork   □ 225g/8oz bamboo shoots   □ 1 courgette   □ 2 tbsps oil   □ 1 spring onion, chopped   □ 100ml/4 fl oz chicken stock   □ 1 tbsp soy sauce   □ 1 tsp cornflour, combined with a little water   □ Salt and pepper

1. Cut the pork into very thin slices and season with salt and pepper.

2. Cut the bamboo shoots into small squares and blanch in boiling, lightly salted water for 2 minutes. Drain well.

3. Using a sharp knife, peel the courgette thickly lengthwise. Discard the remaining flesh and seeds. Slice the peel thinly.

4. Heat the oil in a wok, add the spring onion and the meat. Stir-fry for 1 minute.

5. Pour off any excess fat and stir in the stock. Add the bamboo shoots and the courgette. Cook gently for 7 minutes.

6. Stir in the soy sauce and add the cornflour gradually, stirring continuously until the sauce has thickened. Add salt and pepper to taste. Serve hot.

□ TIME   Preparation takes about 10 minutes and cooking takes approximately 15 minutes.

□ COOK'S TIP   It is very important to blanch the bamboo shoots first to remove bitterness.

□ ECONOMY   The inner part of the courgette could be saved and used for another recipe, such as a purée.

□

OPPOSITE

PORK WITH
BAMBOO SHOOTS

────── SERVES 4 ──────

PORK WITH CHINESE VEGETABLES

*Marinated pork, stir-fried with mushrooms and bamboo shoots
and served in a ginger and garlic flavoured sauce.*

Step 2

Step 2

Step 2

☐ 450g/1lb pork fillet   ☐ ½ tsp chopped garlic   ☐ ½ tsp chopped
fresh ginger root   ☐ ½ tsp cornflour   ☐ Few drops chilli sauce
☐ 1 tbsp wine vinegar   ☐ 225g/8oz bamboo shoots
☐ 1 tbsp soy sauce   ☐ 50g/2oz dried Chinese black mushrooms,
soaked for 15 minutes in warm water   ☐ 2 tbsps oil
☐ 300ml/½ pint chicken stock

1. Cut the pork into small cubes.

2. Place the garlic and ginger on top of the cubed meat. Sprinkle over the cornflour. Add a few drops of chilli sauce, but not too much as it is very hot, then the vinegar. Finally sprinkle over the soy sauce. The meat should now be left to marinate for 20 minutes at room temperature.

3. Cut the bamboo shoots into thin strips, blanch them in boiling, lightly salted water, rinse in cold water and set aside to drain.

4. Rinse the mushrooms and set aside to drain.

5. Remove the meat from the marinade with a slotted spoon. Reserve the marinade.

6. Heat the oil in a wok and sauté the meat. Pour off the excess fat and pour in the stock.

7. Stir in first the mushrooms and the bamboo shoots and then the marinade and cook together until thickened. Serve hot.

☐ TIME   Marinating takes about 20 minutes, preparation takes about 10 minutes and cooking takes approximately 10 minutes.

☐ COOK'S TIP   Since the marinade contains cornflour, the sauce will thicken when cooked. Stir continuously to prevent lumps forming.

☐

OPPOSITE

PORK WITH
CHINESE
VEGETABLES

PORK WITH SCRAMBLED EGGS

*Oyster flavoured scrambled eggs with stir-fried pork
and Chinese mushrooms.*

Step 1

Step 4

Step 4

□ 8 eggs   □ ½ onion, chopped   □ 1 tbsp oyster sauce   □ Salt and pepper   □ 450g/1lb lean pork   □ 2 tbsps oil   □ ½ tsp chopped garlic   □ 30g/1oz dried black Chinese mushrooms, soaked for 15 minutes in warm water   □ 1 tsp sugar   □ ½ tsp soy sauce   □ 200ml/⅓ pint chicken stock   □ 1 tsp cornflour, combined with a little water

1. Beat the eggs together with the onion, oyster sauce and a little pepper. Set aside.

2. Cut the meat into very thin slices.

3. Rinse and drain the mushrooms.

4. Cook the eggs over a very gentle heat in a frying pan, stirring constantly with a wooden spoon or a spatula. This should take approximately 10 minutes.

5. Heat the oil in a wok and sauté the garlic and the pork. Pour off any excess fat and add the mushrooms, sugar, soy sauce and the stock. Cook until the meat is cooked through. Thicken with the cornflour, adding it gradually and stirring continuously until the sauce thickens.

6. Place a bed of scrambled eggs on a warm plate and arrange the meat mixture over the eggs.

□ TIME   Preparation takes about 10 minutes, soaking the mushrooms takes 15 minutes and cooking takes approximately 30 minutes.

□ VARIATION   Add 1 tbsp of chopped fresh chives to the egg mixture before cooking, and sprinkle a little more over the finished dish. Any other herb could also be used.

□ COOK'S TIP   The cooking time for the scrambled eggs will depend on whether you prefer them cooked soft or dry.

□

OPPOSITE

PORK WITH
SCRAMBLED
EGGS

———— SERVES 4 ————

PORK FRITTERS

Stir-fried pork, dipped in a light batter and deep-fried.

Step 2

Step 2

□ 400g/14oz pork tenderloin   □ 2 tbsps oil   □ 150g/6oz flour
□ 1½ tsps baking powder   □ 1 tsp grated lemon zest, blanched in
boiling water   □ 1 egg, beaten   □ 100ml/4 fl oz milk   □ Oil for
deep-frying   □ Salt and pepper

1. Cut the meat into thin slices or small cubes. Heat the oil in a wok and stir-fry the meat until almost cooked, which should take approximately 2 minutes. Drain and set aside.

2. Place the flour in a mixing bowl, add the baking powder and the lemon zest. Beat in the egg and the milk to form a smooth batter.

3. Heat the oil for deep-frying to 180°C/350°F.

4. Dip the slices or cubes of meat into the batter and lower into the preheated oil.

5. Fry until puffy and golden, then drain on kitchen paper. Serve hot, seasoned with salt and pepper.

□ TIME   Preparation takes about 15 minutes and cooking, depending on how many batches you have to fry, takes approximately 35 minutes.

□ SERVING IDEA   If you can obtain them, serve with courgette flowers, also dipped into the batter and deep-fried.

□ CHECKPOINT   Do not heat the oil over 180°C/370°F, or the batter will be done before the pork is cooked through.

□

OPPOSITE

PORK FRITTERS

STUFFED CHINESE LEAVES

These rolls are stuffed with a highly-flavoured meat and vegetable mixture and served in a fragrant sauce.

Step 4

Step 4

Step 4

□ 225g/8oz lean pork   □ 225g/8oz boneless chicken
□ 100g/4oz Chinese leaves   □ 1 tbsp oil   □ ½ tsp chopped garlic
□ 100g/4oz bean sprouts, blanched   □ 2 tbsps canned sweetcorn
□ 2 tbsps soy sauce   □ Salt and pepper   □ 400ml/¾ pint duck stock
□ 1 tsp cornflour, combined with a little water

---

1. Chop the pork and the chicken finely.

2. Reserve 8 Chinese leaves. Shred the remaining leaves finely. Blanch the reserved leaves in boiling water, until soft, then refresh them in cold water and dry on a tea towel.

3. Heat the oil and stir-fry the meat, garlic, shredded Chinese leaves, bean sprouts, sweetcorn, 1 tbsp of the soy sauce, salt and pepper for several minutes.

4. Spread out the blanched leaves and place a small amount of stuffing on each one. Roll up the leaf around the stuffing, beginning at the base and folding in the sides halfway up.

5. Heat together the stock and the remaining soy sauce. Put the stuffed rolls into the stock and cook for 5 minutes, turning occasionally.

6. Remove the rolls and place them on a heated serving plate.

7. Thicken the sauce by adding the cornflour. Heat, stirring continuously, until the sauce thickens. Adjust the seasoning as necessary.

8. To serve, surround the rolls with the sauce, flavoured with a few drops of soy sauce.

□ TIME   Preparation takes about 30 minutes and cooking takes approximately 15 minutes.

□ SERVING IDEA   Wrap a thin strip of blanched leek around each roll, sealing the leek to it with a little beaten egg.

□ CHECKPOINT   If the Chinese leaves are small, you will need to set aside 2 leaves per roll, making a total of 16 leaves, and overlap them around the stuffing.

□

OPPOSITE

STUFFED
CHINESE LEAVES

SERVES 4

MEATBALLS WITH BAMBOO SHOOTS

Stir-fried meatballs with herbs and vegetables,
served in a richly flavoured sauce.

Step 3

Step 3

□ 225g/8oz lean pork   □ 225g/8oz boneless chicken
□ 1 clove garlic, chopped   □ 1 tbsp chopped chives   □ 1 egg
□ Salt and pepper   □ 400g/14oz bamboo shoots   □ 2 tbsps oil
□ 1 spring onion, chopped   □ ½ tsp chopped fresh ginger root
□ 150ml/6 fl oz chicken stock   □ 1 tsp cornflour, combined
with a little water

1. Mince the chicken and pork in a food processor with half of the garlic and chives.

2. Place the meat in a bowl and add the egg. Beat well with a fork. Season with salt and pepper.

3. Cut the bamboo shoots into thin, even slices and blanch in boiling, salted water. Rinse under cold water and drain.

4. Heat 1 tbsp of the oil in a frying pan. Mould the meat in your hands to form small, flat rounds and fry on both sides until almost cooked.

5. Heat the remaining oil in a wok and stir-fry the spring onion, remaining garlic and chives, the ginger and bamboo shoots for 2 minutes.

6. Stir in the chicken stock and allow to reduce. Season again with salt and pepper. Add the diluted cornflour, stirring continuously until the sauce thickens.

7. Cut the meat rounds into even-sized strips and finish cooking in a Chinese steamer.

8. Serve the meat with the bamboo shoots and sauce.

□ TIME   Preparation takes about 25 minutes and cooking takes approximately 40 minutes.

□ VARIATION   Use any meat for this recipe.

□ COOK'S TIP   The meat rounds are rather fragile; turn them over carefully so as not to break them. You may use a small plate as a support when turning them over.

□

OPPOSITE

MEATBALLS
WITH BAMBOO
SHOOTS

—— SERVES 4 ——

BEEF WITH ONIONS

*Marinated beef, sautéed with onions, garlic and ginger
and served in a smooth sauce.*

Step 5

Step 6

☐ 450g/1lb fillet steak

MARINADE

☐ 1 tbsp oil   ☐ 1 tsp sesame oil   ☐ 1 tbsp Chinese wine
☐ 1 tbsp oil   ☐ 1 piece fresh ginger root, peeled and roughly
chopped   ☐ 3 onions, finely sliced   ☐ 1 garlic clove, chopped
☐ 300ml/½ pint beef stock   ☐ 1 pinch of sugar   ☐ 2 tbsps dark
soy sauce   ☐ 1 tsp cornflour, combined with a little water
☐ Salt and pepper

1. Cut the fillet into very thin slices.

2. Mix together the marinade ingredients and stir in the meat. Leave to marinate for 30 minutes.

3. Heat 1 tbsp oil in a wok and sauté the ginger, onions and garlic until lightly browned.

4. Lift the meat out of the marinade with a slotted spoon and discard the marinade. Add the meat to the wok and sauté with the vegetables.

5. Pour over the stock, sugar and soy sauce. Cook for 4 minutes.

6. Thicken the sauce with the cornflour, stirring continuously until the desired consistency is reached. Season with salt and pepper and serve immediately.

☐ TIME   Preparation takes about 15 minutes and cooking takes approximately 20 minutes.

☐ SERVING IDEA   Serve this dish on a bed of boiled or steamed white rice.

☐ CHECKPOINT   If you use a wok, watch the cooking process carefully, as the ingredients cook very quickly.

☐

OPPOSITE

BEEF WITH ONIONS

STIR-FRIED BEEF
WITH PINEAPPLE

*Sliced fillet steak cooked with pineapple and served
in a sweet, pungent sauce.*

Step 2

Step 2

Step 3

☐ 450g/1lb fillet steak ☐ ½ fresh pineapple ☐ 1 tbsp oil
☐ 1 spring onion, chopped ☐ ½ tsp chopped fresh ginger root
☐ 1 tsp vinegar ☐ 1 tsp sugar ☐ 2 tsps light soy sauce
☐ 300ml/½ pint chicken stock ☐ 100ml/4 fl oz pineapple juice
☐ ½ tomato, seeded and chopped ☐ 1 tsp cornflour, combined
with a little water ☐ Salt and pepper

1. Cut the fillet steak into thin strips and season with salt and pepper.

2. Peel the pineapple and cut out all the brown 'eyes' from the flesh.

3. Cut into round slices, removing any tough parts parts and the core.

4. Cut the remaining flesh into small, even pieces.

5. Heat the oil in the wok. Add the onion, ginger and the meat and stir-fry until lightly coloured.

6. Pour off any excess fat.

7. Stir in the vinegar, sugar, soy sauce, chicken stock and pineapple juice. Add the tomato and the pineapple pieces. Reduce the heat and cook for a few minutes.

8. Add the cornflour gradually, stirring continuously until the desired consistency is reached.

☐ TIME Preparation takes about 15 minutes and cooking takes approximately 30 minutes.

☐ VARIATION Fresh pineapple juice could be used. Liquidize the remaining ½ pineapple and then pass it through a sieve. Make up to 100ml/4 fl oz with water if necessary.

☐ CHECKPOINT Cornflour can be used to thicken many sauces, but always stir it in gradually, so that the sauce does not thicken too much.

☐

OPPOSITE

STIR-FRIED BEEF
WITH PINEAPPLE

--- SERVES 4 ---

BEEF IN OYSTER SAUCE

Marinated beef, cooked and served in a ginger and oyster sauce.

Step 4

Step 5

☐ 1 tbsp sake ☐ ½ tsp bicarbonate of soda ☐ ½ tsp sugar ☐ 450g/1lb fillet steak, cut into thin slices ☐ 2 tbsps oil ☐ 1 spring onion, chopped ☐ ½ tsp chopped garlic ☐ ½ tsp chopped fresh ginger root ☐ 1 tbsp green peppercorns ☐ 2 tbsps oyster sauce ☐ 300ml/½ pint beef stock ☐ 1 tsp cornflour, combined with a little water ☐ Salt and pepper

1. Mix together the sake, bicarbonate of soda and the sugar. Place the sliced meat in the marinade and marinate at room temperature for 1 hour.

2. When the meat is ready to cook, heat the oil in a wok and briefly stir-fry the spring onion, garlic, ginger and peppercorns.

3. Drain the meat, reserving the marinade.

4. Add the drained meat to the wok, stir well and cook for 1 minute. Pour off any excess oil.

5. Pour over the marinade, stir in the oyster sauce and the beef stock. Season well with salt and pepper.

6. Allow the sauce to reduce slightly. If it is still too thin, add a little of the cornflour, stirring continously until the desired consistency is reached.

☐ TIME   Preparation takes about 20 minutes and cooking takes approximately 15 minutes.

☐ VARIATION   If green peppercorns are not available, use the mixed variety, but reduce the quantity by half.

☐ CHECKPOINT   This dish should be cooked rapidly, so that the meat does not dry out.

☐

OPPOSITE

BEEF IN OYSTER SAUCE

----------- SERVES 4 -----------

BEEF WITH BROCCOLI

A slightly hot sauce accompanies this dish of beef and broccoli.

Step 5

Step 5

Step 7

□ 600g/1½lbs rib of beef   □ 225g/8oz broccoli   □ 1 tbsp oil
□ 1-inch piece fresh ginger root, peeled and finely chopped
□ 1 tbsp sake   □ 2 tsps chilli sauce   □ 350ml/12 fl oz beef stock
□ 2 tbsps dark soy sauce   □ Salt and pepper   □ 1 tsp cornflour,
combined with a little water

1. Cut the beef into small cubes. Do not remove any fat from the meat.

2. Cut off the hard stem from the broccoli and separate the florets. The stems may be reserved for another dish, such as a broccoli purée.

3. Bring a large quantity of salted water to the boil. Add the broccoli florets and cook until tender but still slightly crisp. Rinse immediately under cold water to stop the cooking process and then leave to drain.

4. Heat the oil in a wok and stir-fry the ginger and the meat.

5. Pour off any excess fat and deglaze the wok with the sake. Stir in the chilli sauce, beef stock and the soy sauce. Cook over a gentle heat for 10 minutes.

6. Remove the meat with a slotted spoon and keep warm. Season the sauce with salt and pepper to taste.

7. Add the well-drained broccoli to the wok, allowing it to heat through completely. Remove with a slotted spoon and keep warm with the meat.

8. Add the cornflour to the sauce in the wok, stirring continuously until the desired consistency is reached.

9. Serve the meat and broccoli topped with the sauce.

□ TIME   Preparation takes about 20 minutes and cooking takes approximately 25 minutes.

□ VARIATION   Replace the broccoli with cauliflower florets.

□ CHECKPOINT   If you think there will not be enough sauce, add a little more beef stock before you thicken it with the cornflour.

□

OPPOSITE

BEEF WITH
BROCCOLI

BEEF WITH CHINESE MUSHROOMS

*Unlike most Chinese meat dishes, this one does not have a sauce.
The beef is first marinated and then simply
dry-cooked with the mushrooms.*

Step 1

Step 1

Step 1

☐ 1 tsp cornflour   ☐ 1 tbsp light soy sauce   ☐ 1 egg white
☐ 1 tsp sugar   ☐ 450g/1lb rump steak, thinly sliced   ☐ 6 dried
Chinese black mushrooms, soaked for 1 hour in warm water
☐ 2 tbsps light soy sauce   ☐ ½ tsp chopped garlic
☐ Salt and pepper   ☐ 2 tbsps Chinese wine

1. To make this unusual marinade, begin by placing the cornflour in a small bowl. Stir in the soy sauce. Now beat in the egg white and the sugar, beating thoroughly to combine all the ingredients. Add the slices of beef and leave to marinate for 1 hour.

2. Drain the mushrooms, which should be very soft. Cut them into thin strips.

3. Transfer the beef from the marinade to a small plate, without draining.

4. Heat the oil in a wok, stir-fry the garlic, beef and the mushrooms until coloured. Season with salt and pepper.

5. Stir in the wine and serve as soon as it has evaporated.

☐ TIME   Pre-soak the mushrooms for 1 hour. Marinating the beef takes 1 hour, preparation about 20 minutes and cooking takes approximately 10 minutes.

☐ SERVING IDEA   Serve with plain steamed rice or stir-fried rice and vegetables.

☐

OPPOSITE

BEEF WITH
CHINESE
MUSHROOMS

SERVES 4

BEEF WITH GINGER SAUCE

Quick-fried beef with fresh ginger root, served in
a soy and tomato sauce.

□ 450g/1lb fillet of beef   □ 2 tbsps oil   □ 2 tbsps fresh ginger root,
peeled and cut into small matchsticks   □ 2 tomatoes, peeled, seeded
and finely chopped   □ 1 tsp sugar   □ 1 tbsp red wine vinegar
□ 2 tbsps soy sauce   □ Salt and pepper

Step 2

Step 3

1. Cut the beef into very thin slices.

2. Heat the oil in a wok, add the meat and the ginger and stir-fry for 1 minute.

3. Pour off any excess fat, and stir in the tomato. Reduce the heat and add the sugar, vinegar and the soy sauce.

4. Cook for a few minutes to allow the flavours to develop, then season with salt and pepper to taste and serve immediately.

□ TIME   Preparation takes about 10 minutes and cooking takes approximately 5 minutes.

□ SERVING IDEA   Serve with tomatoes, lightly seasoned with salt and pepper and heated through in a steamer.

□ CHECKPOINT   Do not allow the ginger to cook for too long, or its flavour will be spoiled.

□

OPPOSITE

BEEF WITH
GINGER SAUCE

SERVES 4

STIR-FRIED LAMB WITH SESAME SEEDS

Lightly caramelized lamb, served on a bed of sautéed onions with a sesame seed flavoured sauce.

Step 1

Step 1

□ 2 tbsps oil □ 600g/1lb 6oz shoulder of lamb, boned □ 2 onions, thinly sliced □ ½ clove garlic, chopped □ 100ml/4 fl oz lamb stock or other meat stock □ 1 tsp sugar □ 1 tbsp soy sauce □ ½ tsp wine vinegar □ Salt and pepper □ 1 tbsp sesame seeds

1. Cut away any excess fat from the lamb. Slice the meat very thinly, using a sharp knife. Heat the oil in a wok and stir-fry the lamb. Remove when cooked and set aside.

2. In the same oil, fry the onions and garlic. Once they have become transparent, remove them and set aside.

3. Pour off any excess fat and put the meat back in the wok with the lamb stock, sugar, soy sauce and vinegar. Continue cooking until the sauce is reduced. Season to taste with salt and pepper.

4. When the meat is lightly caramelized, sprinkle over the sesame seeds and stir. Serve hot on a bed of the sautéed onions.

□ TIME   Preparation takes about 10 minutes and cooking takes approximately 20 minutes.

□ VARIATION   Use any cut of lamb, cutting away any excess fat, before slicing very thinly.

□ CHECKPOINT   This recipe is served without sauce. As the meat is caramelized, it should stay moist.

□

OPPOSITE

STIR-FRIED
LAMB WITH
SESAME SEEDS

LAMBS' KIDNEYS WITH ASPARAGUS

*Gently fried lambs' kidneys cooked in a sweet, spicy sauce
and served with asparagus tips.*

Step 2

Step 2

Step 2

☐ 12 green asparagus spears ☐ 4 lambs' kidneys ☐ Salt and pepper
☐ 100g/4oz small dried black Chinese mushrooms, soaked for
15 minutes in warm water ☐ 2 tbsps oil ☐ 1 shallot, chopped
☐ 1 tsp dark soy sauce ☐ 1 tbsp hoisin sauce ☐ 200ml/7 fl oz
chicken stock ☐ Few drops chilli sauce

1. Peel and trim the asparagus and cook in boiling, lightly salted water until tender. Rinse in cold water and set aside to drain.

2. Buy kidneys which are of about the same size so that they cook evenly throughout. Cut the kidneys in half, cutting out any nerves and gristle. Season with salt and pepper.

3. Cook the mushrooms for about 10 minutes in a small quantity of boiling water. Rinse them in cold water and set aside to drain.

4. Heat the oil in a wok and cook the kidneys for approximately 3 minutes. Remove them and place on a tea towel or kitchen paper so that the blood is absorbed.

5. Pour off any excess fat from the wok and add the shallot, soy sauce, hoisin sauce, mushrooms, stock and chilli sauce. Cook for 2 minutes.

6. Return the kidneys to the wok and cook until the sauce is slightly reduced.

7. Adjust the seasoning, adding salt and pepper to taste.

8. Reheat the asparagus by steaming lightly. Serve hot, with the kidneys in their sauce.

☐ TIME   Preparation takes about 10 minutes and cooking takes approximately 35 minutes.

☐ VARIATION   Green asparagus is usually the first to come in season, followed by the white variety. Use whichever is available.

☐ COOK'S TIP   It is very important to leave the kidneys to drain completely on a tea towel or kitchen paper. They contain a lot of blood which might otherwise run during cooking (Step 6) and ruin the flavour of the dish.

☐

OPPOSITE

LAMBS' KIDNEYS
WITH ASPARAGUS

SERVES 4

LAMB WITH TRANSPARENT NOODLES

Quick-fried lamb, coated in a light, soy-based sauce and served with transparent noodles.

Step 4

Step 5

Step 6

☐ 450g/1lb lean lamb ☐ 100g/4oz transparent noodles ☐ 2 tbsps oil ☐ 1 tsp chopped garlic ☐ 1 spring onion, chopped ☐ 2 tbsps soy sauce ☐ 200ml/7 fl oz lamb stock ☐ Salt and pepper

1. Cut the meat into thin slices.

2. Bring a large quantity of salted water to the boil. Add the noodles and cook them for approximately 45 seconds. Rinse immediately in cold water and set aside to drain.

3. Heat the oil in a wok and stir-fry the garlic and spring onion.

4. Add the meat slices to the wok and stir-fry for 1 minute.

5. Stir in the soy sauce and the stock and cook over a gentle heat until the meat is cooked through.

6. Add the well-drained noodles and allow to heat through. Adjust the seasoning, adding salt and pepper as necessary. Serve hot.

☐ TIME   Preparation takes about 10 minutes and cooking takes approximately 15 minutes.

☐ CHECKPOINT   Once the stock has been added to the wok, reduce the heat and finish cooking very slowly so that the stock does not evaporate.

☐ SERVING IDEA   Serve with steamed mange tout.

☐

OPPOSITE

LAMB WITH TRANSPARENT NOODLES

SAUTÉED FRUIT SALAD

*In this unusual fruit salad, the exotic ingredients are stir-fried in
a little oil and delicately flavoured with cinnamon.*

Step 1

Step 2

☐ 4 slices fresh pineapple   ☐ 4 jackfruit or breadfruit   ☐ 6 palm fruit
☐ 1 grapefruit   ☐ 1 pear   ☐ ½ mango   ☐ 12 lychees, peeled
☐ 2 tbsps oil   ☐ 2 tbsps sugar   ☐ Ground cinnamon

1. Cut the pineapple, jackfruit or breadfruit and palm fruit into thin slices. Peel the grapefruit and cut into segments. Peel the pear and the mango, and cut both into thin slices.

2. Heat the oil and stir-fry the fruit in the following order: pineapple, lychees, jackfruit or breadfruit, mango, pears, palm fruit and lastly the grapefruit. Sprinkle with the sugar. Cook for a few more minutes and sprinkle with the cinnamon.

3. Serve either hot or cold.

☐ TIME   Preparation takes about 30 minutes and cooking takes approximately 10 minutes.

☐ VARIATION   Add a few strawberries once all the fruit is cooked.

☐ COOK'S TIP   Vary the mixture of fruit according to season and availability, but always stir-fry the most fragile fruit last, to retain its shape and texture.

☐

OPPOSITE

SAUTÉED FRUIT
SALAD

----- SERVES 4 -----

KUMQUATS WITH CRYSTALLIZED GINGER

If you serve this dessert to guests with a sweet tooth,
you just cannot go wrong!

Step 1

Step 2

□ 20 kumquats   □ 1-inch piece fresh ginger root, peeled and sliced
□ 225g/8oz sugar

1. Using a brush, clean the kumquats. Blanch them in boiling water and drain. Blanch the ginger root slices in boiling water and drain in turn.

2. Place the blanched kumquats in a saucepan with the sugar. Cover with water to a height of 5cm/2 inches above the fruit. Add the sliced ginger and bring to the boil.

3. Reduce the heat and allow the liquid to reduce and caramelize gently. This is a long process, taking about 1½ hours. Add a little more water during cooking, if necessary.

4. Allow the dish to cool after cooking and then chill in the refrigerator. Cut the ginger into very small pieces before serving.

□ TIME   Preparation takes about 20 minutes and cooking takes approximately 2 hours.

□ SERVING IDEA   Cook the two ingredients separately, in case one of your guests does not like the flavour of one of the ingredients.

□ CHECKPOINT   The cooking should be done very slowly, so that the sugar penetrates to the very centre of the kumquats.

□

OPPOSITE

KUMQUATS WITH
CRYSTALLIZED
GINGER

———— SERVES 4 ————

RICE PUDDINGS WITH CRYSTALLIZED FRUIT

These puddings have a very unusual flavour, a little strange to Western palates, but tasty nonetheless!

Step 5

Step 5

Step 5

☐ 300g/10oz glutinous rice ☐ 4 tbsps sugar ☐ 75g/3oz crystallized fruit, chopped ☐ 2 drops bitter almond essence ☐ 20 dates, stoned ☐ 1 tsp oil, warmed

1. Rinse the rice first in cold then in hot water. Place in a saucepan and cover with water to a height of 1 cm/½ inch above the top of the rice, bring to the boil and cook, stirring occasionally. Once the rice is almost cooked, remove the pan from the heat. The rice will finish cooking in the hot water by itself.

2. Stir in the sugar, crystallized fruit and almond essence. Set aside to cool.

3. Place the dates in a food processor and blend until a smooth, solid paste forms.

4. Using your fingers, work this paste into 4 flat, even circles to fit individual moulds.

5. Grease 4 individual moulds with the warmed oil and place a layer of rice in the bottom. Place a date circle on top and finish with another layer of rice.

6. Cook the moulds in a steamer for 30 minutes, to allow the flavours to mix and develop. Allow to cool and then chill in the refrigerator before serving.

☐ TIME Preparation takes about 45 minutes and cooking takes 30 minutes. Cooking the glutinous rice takes about 20 minutes.

☐ VARIATION Cook the rice in milk instead of water. Add a little chopped crystallized ginger to the rice mixture.

☐

OPPOSITE

RICE PUDDINGS
WITH
CRYSTALLIZED
FRUIT

MELON SALAD

*A refreshing fruit salad, which is especially tasty served after
a heavy meal of many courses.*

Step 1

Step 1

☐ 1 large cantaloupe melon   ☐ 1 mango   ☐ 4 canned lychees
☐ 4 large or 8 small strawberries   ☐ Lychee syrup from the can

1. Peel and seed the melon and cut into thin slices.

2. Peel and stone the mango and cut into thin slices.

3. Using a melon baller, cut as many balls as possible out of the strawberries.

4. Arrange the melon slices evenly on 4 small plates.

5. Spread a layer of mango over the melon. Place a lychee in the centre of each plate and arrange a few strawberry balls around the edges.

6. Divide the lychee syrup evenly between the plates of fruit and chill them in the refrigerator before serving.

☐ TIME   Preparation takes about 30 minutes.

☐ VARIATION   Use a honeydew melon instead of the cantaloupe variety.

☐ COOK'S TIP   This dessert is best served well-chilled from the refrigerator, so prepare it several hours in advance of serving.

☐

OPPOSITE

MELON SALAD

STUFFED LYCHEES

*Mouthwatering lychees, stuffed with a mixture
of dates and bananas.*

Step 2

Step 3

Step 3

☐ 10 dates, stoned ☐ 2 bananas ☐ Juice of ½ lemon
☐ 20 canned lychees, reserving a little syrup for the sauce

1. Place the stoned dates in a food processor and blend until a thick paste forms.

2. Peel and mash the bananas with the lemon juice. Add the date paste and mix together well.

3. Place the mixture in a piping bag and use to stuff the lychees.

4. Mix the lychee syrup into the leftover stuffing to make a sauce. Serve the stuffed, chilled lychees with the sauce.

☐ TIME   Preparation takes about 30 minutes.

☐ VARIATION   You could use fresh lychees, which should be stoned before stuffing. Make a syrup with equal parts of water and sugar lightly boiled together, to replace the lychee syrup from the can.

☐ CHECKPOINT   The lemon is a very necessary addition to prevent the bananas turning black.

☐

OPPOSITE

STUFFED
LYCHEES

——— SERVES 4 ———

DATE DUMPLINGS

*Light and puffy, these steamed date dumplings are delicious served
with a raspberry sauce.*

Step 1

Step 2

Step 2

☐ 150ml/5 fl oz water   ☐ 150ml/5 fl oz milk   ☐ 2 tsps baking
powder   ☐ 1 tbsp sugar   ☐ 1 pinch salt   ☐ 400g/14oz plain flour,
sieved   ☐ 15 dates, stoned   ☐ 1 tbsp ground almonds

1. Mix together the water and the milk. Incorporate the baking powder, sugar and salt.

2. Stirring well, incorporate the flour gradually into the above mixture, forming it into a ball. You may find it easier to use your fingers, rather than a spoon.

3. Let the dough rest in a warm place for 1 hour.

4. Place the dates and the almonds in a food processor and blend until a smooth paste is formed.

5. On a lightly floured surface, roll out small lumps of the dough into circles.

6. Place a little of the date mixture in the centre of each circle. Pull the edges up over the top, pinching them together well with your fingers to seal. Roll in your hands to form small balls.

7. Steam the dumplings for approximately 20 minutes. You may need to do this in more than one batch.

8. Serve hot or cold.

☐ TIME   Preparation takes about 1 hour 20 minutes and cooking takes approximately 20 minutes per batch.

☐ SERVING IDEA   Serve the dumplings with a raspberry sauce. Crush fresh raspberries and add sieved icing sugar to taste. Mix together well and serve.

☐ CHECKPOINT   Make sure that you pinch the edges of the dumplings together firmly with your fingers before rolling them into balls.

☐

OPPOSITE

DATE
DUMPLINGS

'HALF-MOON' BANANA PASTRIES

*These crunchy pastries are rather dry, and are traditionally served
with a cup of Chinese tea.*

Step 1

Step 1

PASTRY

□ 450g/1lb plain flour, sieved □ 100g/4oz lard □ Pinch salt
□ 100ml/4 fl oz water

FILLING

□ 3 bananas □ 2 tsps sugar □ Pinch cinnamon □ Few drops of
lemon juice □ 1 egg yolk, beaten

1. Rub the lard into the flour with the salt. Using your fingers, incorporate the water gradually to form a ball. Wrap a damp cloth around the pastry and leave it to rest in a cool place for 30 minutes.

2. Peel and crush the bananas with a fork. Add the sugar, cinnamon and lemon juice. Mix together well.

3. Roll out small pieces of pastry on a lightly floured surface, and cut into circles. Place a little of the banana filling on each round of pastry. Fold into half-moon shapes and seal the edges first by pinching together with your fingers and then by decorating with a fork.

4. Continue until all the pastry and filling have been used.

5. Brush the beaten egg yolk over the half-moon pastries. Pierce the pastry once to allow steam to escape during cooking. Cook in a moderate oven, 180°C/350°F/Gas Mark 4, for approximately 20 minutes, until crisp and golden.

□ TIME   Preparation takes about 25 minutes, resting time for the pastry is 30 minutes and cooking takes approximately 20 minutes.

□ VARIATION   Make up the pastries using different fruit fillings.

□ COOK'S TIP   The cooked pastry in this recipe is very crisp. Serve the pastries with a fruit drink in summer and hot Chinese tea in winter.

□ CHECKPOINT   Be sure to seal the edges of the pastries thoroughly so that no filling escapes during cooking.

□

OPPOSITE

'HALF-MOON'
BANANA
PASTRIES

─── SERVES 4 ───

ALMOND JELLY

A smooth almond jelly, which is very tasty served with
fresh lychees or half-moon pastries.

Step 2

Step 2

Step 3

□ 300ml/½ pint milk   □ 3 sheets gelatine, pre-soaked in cold water, or 1 packet powdered gelatine, soaked in 1 tbsp water
□ 25g/1oz ground almonds   □ 5 drops almond essence
□ 50g/2oz sugar   □ 1 tin lychees

1. Heat the milk in a saucepan until hot, but not boiling.

2. Drain the pre-soaked gelatine sheets very carefully, if using. They should not drip water during the next step. Stir the gelatine into the hot milk.

3. Stir in the ground almonds, almond essence and sugar.

4. Stir well, until the gelatine has dissolved. Using a wire whisk will make the job easier.

5. Pour the liquid jelly into a soup plate and leave in the refrigerator for at least 2 hours until set.

6. Once the jelly has set, turn it out onto a cutting board and cut into slices, or any other shapes.

7. Place the slices on a serving plate, decorate with the lychees and pour over a little of the juice from the tin.

□ TIME   Preparation takes about 1 hour and it takes at least 2 hours for the jelly to set.

□ CHECKPOINT   If you have trouble removing the jelly from the soup plate, cut it into slices whilst still in the plate. Remove a few of the slices and give the plate a good shake. The remaining jelly should then come loose.

□

OPPOSITE

ALMOND JELLY

---— SERVES 4 ——---

RICE IN MILK

This is delicious served either hot or cold.

Step 3

Step 4

□ 75g/3oz long grain rice   □ 600ml/1 pint milk   □ 1 tbsp clear honey   □ ¼ tsp ground cinnamon   □ 5 cubes sugar

1. Blanch the rice in boiling water, rinse well and set aside to drain.

2. Pour the milk into a saucepan and stir in the honey.

3. Sprinkle in the cinnamon.

4. Stir in the well-drained rice and the sugar cubes. Cook over a gentle heat, stirring from time to time.

5. Once the rice has absorbed all the liquid, remove from the heat.

6. Serve either hot or cold.

□ TIME   Preparation takes about 10 minutes and cooking takes approximately 20 minutes, but can vary according to the quality of the rice. Remove from the heat as soon as all the liquid has been absorbed.

□ SERVING IDEA   Allow the rice to cool before chilling in the refrigerator. Scoop out balls of the chilled rice with an ice cream scoop and serve with a fresh raspberry coulis.

□ VARIATION   The rice can be cooked in the oven in a covered casserole. If so, it is very important to monitor the level of the liquid, and to remove the casserole as soon as the rice has absorbed all the liquid.

□

OPPOSITE

RICE IN MILK

---- SERVES 4 ----

KIWI AND COCONUT DUO

*Incredibly simple to prepare, this recipe is a delicious blend of
kiwi fruit, fresh coconut and coconut milk.*

Step 2

Step 3

☐ 4 kiwi fruit ☐ 1 fresh coconut ☐ A little sugar (optional)

1. Remove the stalks from the ends of the kiwis.

2. Peel them lengthwise with a small sharp knife.

3. Slice them thinly widthways.

4. Cut the coconut into pieces, reserving all the milk.

5. Cut the coconut flesh into very thin slices.

6. Arrange the kiwi slices on a serving plate and surround with the slices of coconut.

7. Add a little sugar to the coconut milk if desired and pour over the fruit. Serve chilled.

☐ TIME Preparation takes about 25 minutes.

☐ VARIATION Coconut milk can now be bought in tins. It is usually of very high quality and is thicker than fresh coconut milk.

☐ COOK'S TIP The addition of sugar to the milk is optional, and depends upon the acidity of the milk.

☐

OPPOSITE

**KIWI AND
COCONUT DUO**

SERVES 4

PEANUT BUTTER CAKE

This peanut butter cake is light but nonetheless quite filling and is very good served chilled.

□ 125g/5oz margarine, softened to room temperature □ 75g/3oz sugar □ 4 eggs, separated and the whites stiffly whisked □ 100g/4oz plain flour, sieved □ Pinch salt □ 2 tbsps smooth peanut butter □ 1 tsp vanilla sugar, or ½ tsp vanilla essence + 1 tsp sugar □ 1 tsp grated lemon peel

Step 1

Step 2

Step 4

Step 5

1. Beat or whisk together the softened margarine and the sugar until light and fluffy.

2. Add the egg yolks and beat them in well.

3. Beat in the sieved flour and the salt.

4. Add the peanut butter, vanilla sugar and the lemon peel. Beat well to combine all the ingredients.

5. Using a metal spoon or rubber spatula, gently fold half the egg whites into the mixture.

6. Gently fold in the remaining egg whites. Pour the cake mixture into a nonstick baking tin and cook in a moderate oven, 180°C/350°F/Gas Mark 4, until the cake has risen slightly and is firm to the touch.

7. Allow to cool, before removing from the tin. Serve either slightly warm or chilled.

□ TIME Preparation takes about 15 minutes and cooking takes approximately 30 minutes.

□ SERVING IDEA Cut the cake into decorative shapes using a sharp knife or biscuit cutter and serve with a kiwi coulis, sweetened to taste with a little sugar.

□ COOK'S TIP Fold in the egg whites as described. If they are whisked in, the mixture will fall.

□

OPPOSITE

PEANUT
BUTTER CAKE

---- SERVES 4 ----

EXOTIC FRUIT SALAD

*Fresh fruit marinated in orange and lychee juice
with just a hint of almond.*

Step 1

Step 1

Step 1

☐ 1 papaya   ☐ 1 pomegranate   ☐ 2 kiwi fruit   ☐ 4 rambutan fruit
☐ 4 canned lychees, plus the juice from the can   ☐ 3 blood oranges
☐ 3 drops bitter almond essence, or ordinary almond essence

1. Peel all the fruit except the oranges, removing pips or stones as necessary. Try to buy a fully ripe papaya for the salad. Cut it in half. Using a small spoon, remove all the pips and any stringy skin around them. Peel each half, but not too thickly as the flesh immediately below the skin is very good. Finally, cut the flesh into thin slices or other fancy shapes.

2. Peel two of the oranges. Remove all the pith and cut the flesh into small pieces.

3. Squeeze the juice from the remaining orange, mix this with the canned lychee juice and add the almond essence.

4. Cut all the remaining fruit into slices, rounds or small cubes and combine these with the prepared papaya and oranges in a bowl. Pour over the almond flavoured juices and leave the salad to marinate for a few hours in the refrigerator.

5. Serve chilled.

☐ TIME   Preparation takes about 1 hour and the salad should be left to marinate for at least 3 hours.

☐ SERVING IDEA   Cut a few fresh mint leaves into thin strips to garnish the fruit salad just before serving.

☐ CHECKPOINT   Exotic fruit often arrives in the shops before it is ripe. The solution is to sweeten the sauce slightly before marinating the fruit in order to eliminate acidity.

☐ BUYING GUIDE   If any of the fruits are out of season and unavailable, substitute other appropriate fruit, as desired.

☐

OPPOSITE

**EXOTIC FRUIT
SALAD**